Memoir Of William Burke

MEMOIR

OF

WILLIAM BURKE,

A

SOLDIER OF THE REVOLUTION.

REFORMED FROM INTEMPERANCE, AND FOR MANY
YEARS A CONSISTENT AND DEVOTED
CHRISTIAN.

Carefully prepared from a Journal kept by Himself.

To which is added, an extract from a sermon preached at
his funeral, by Rev. Nathaniel Miner.

HARTFORD.
CASE, TIFFANY, AND COMPANY.
1837.

CERTIFICATE.

This may certify, that we, the undersigned, have, for several years, (and some of us for more than twenty years,) been intimately acquainted with WILLIAM BURKE, late of East Haddam, and from what we have known of his Life and Conversation, we do believe him to have been a sincere and exemplary Christian; and that the little volume containing an account of his life and conversion, may be read with confidence, and we hope with profit, as containing the truth, and all the material facts in his history.

NATHANIEL MINER,
Pastor of the Second Congregatiqnal Church in East Haddam.
DEA. JONATHAN BECKWITH,
DEA. WILLIAM E. CONE,
SAMUEL EMMONS,
JOSEPH W. CONE,
GEORGE RANSOM,
REED ANDERSON,
ERASTUS CONE,
Members of the Church to which Mr. Burke belonged.

MILLINGTON, (East Haddam,) April, 1837.

CONTENTS.

CHAPTER I.

CHAPTER II.

CHAPTER III.

CHAPTER IV.

CHAPTER V.

CHAPTER VI.

CHAPTER VII.

CHAPTER VIII.

CHAPTER IX.

CHAPTER XIV.

CHAPTER XV.

CHAPTER XVI.

CHAPTER XVII.

CHAPTER I.

His birth and education. Enlists in the army; is very active. Embarks for Minorca. Receives orders to sail for America. His conduct up to the time of his desertion in 1778.

I was born in the county of Galway, Ireland, A. D. 1752, and by the death of both my parents, I was left an orphan nine or ten years old. My father died soon after my mother; they were, Roman Catholics. At the time of their death I knew no better than to go to the priest, and confess my sins and receive his absolution; he would tell me that I was then as free from sin as the child unborn. Soon after the death of my father I was sent to school. I became fond of going to school, and at the age of fourteen could read and write very well. About this time, a Mr. James Morrison, a dancing master, came from England, and set up a school in the town where I then lived. I went to his school; he taught reading and writing, as well as dancing. I soon

1

grew very fond of dancing, and made great proficiency in the art.

By this time, I had grown to the size of a man, was 16 or 17 years old, and went to live with Thomas Hudson, Esq., near the town of Aithlone, 65 miles west of the city of Dublin, in the capacity of steward. I collected his laborers, and kept accounts of the number of days they worked, &c. After living with this gentleman two years, I went to live with the Rev. Mr. Young, a clergyman of the Church of England, who lived in the town of Aithlone. With him I lived two years; my employment was the collection of his salary. From thence I went to live with Pierce Fitsgerald, Esq., of Baltimore, within 30 miles of Dublin. At this time the British officers were beating up for volunteers, and as I had a wish to become a soldier, I took a seat in the stage coach for Limerick, where was the 5th regiment of foot, commanded by the Hon. Col. Henry Monckton, who was shortly to sail with his regiment up the straits of Minorca. When I arrived, I went to Col. Monckton and told him who I was, as he had some knowledge of my father's family. I joined his regiment, and soon after this, a soldier having deserted from the regiment, I offered to go as one of the four men whom the colonel was to send with the corporal in pursuit of the man. The colonel smiled and said I might go. So we took

off our scarlet coats, and put on others, to prevent
our being known by the deserter if we should
come where he was. The corporal and the other
three had but little knowledge of the customs and
manners of the Catholic Irish, but I was well
versed in their language, and well acquainted with
their customs. The corporal gave up the command and the management of the business to me.
We had sixty or seventy miles to go among the
wild Irish, and meeting one of the king's tide-
waiters, he told us he believed he knew where the
deserter might be found. We set off directly for
the place which had been pointed out, and arrived
there just at dark. Having lain by till the people
in the house had all retired to rest, I then set a
sentry at each door, and entered the house with
the corporal and one of the men, lighted a candle,
and went to the bed room, where the man of the
house and his sons were lying, and told them if
they made any noise they were dead men; instantly placed a sentinel over them, and went with
the corporal, into the room where the deserter was
in bed with a young woman who had ran away in
his company. I sprung to the bed side, put my
bayonet to his breast, and told him he was my
prisoner. We then took him, and set off for the
river that runs from that place to Limerick; we
had seven or eight miles to march to the place
where we had seen the king's tide-waiter; we

arrived at day-light, and embarked on board a
sloop for Limerick, and arrived there the afternoon of the next day. When we came to the
castle the whole regiment flocked around us to
see the deserter; they had thought that we should
all have been killed by the Catholic Irish. The
colonel ordered the sergeant of the guard to take
the deserter to the guard house; he then thanked
us for our faithfulness, and when he understood
from all the party that young Burke was the sole
means of taking the prisoner, he told me he would
not forget me, and then put his hand into his
pocket, and gave me a guinea. Soon after this,
I was sent to the town of Aithlone in pursuit of
a deserter. I found him and enlisted three or four
young men. When I returned the colonel was
highly pleased, and told me that if I went on as
I had begun, I should soon have a commission.
This was in the autumn of 1774; early the next
April we received orders to be ready for foreign
service, and shortly afterwards we marched to the
city of Cork. We tarried there six days. While
there our regiment was ordered under arms to
guard a man to the gallows; this was the first
time that I had seen a man hung.

On the 12th of May, 1775, we embarked for
Minorca; there were several transports employed
to convey the whole regiment, which was one
thousand strong, besides officers and women and

children. Our voyage was very pleasant till we arrived in the bay of Biscay, where we had such a terrible storm for two days and nights that the captain ordered the hatchway closed down, and tarpauling nailed over it. My situation was now very unpleasant, as I had never been ten miles on the salt water before. I would have given the whole world that I could be on shore, but I had *made my own bed and felt that I must lie on it.*

I begged and prayed for mercy, although I was very ignorant of that holy God upon whom I called. I had been taught to pray in the Catholic manner from a child, and always kept a prayer book. Soon the Lord was pleased to send us calm weather. The ship seemed to work regular; we sailed onward until we came near Gibralter, when one morning, to our great surprise a British man of war came in sight, and fired a great gun over our ship. We did not know what it meant. She soon came up with us and hailed. Our captain answered. She inquired where we were bound. Our captain answered "to Minorca." The commodore asked what troops were on board, and we answered the 45th regiment. "Who commands them?" "The Hon. Col. Monckton." "Tell him to come on board my ship." The colonel went on board the man of war, and was ordered to sail for New York, North America, as the king's colonies had rebelled. So we were all

1*

countermanded. The troops were sorry, but could not help themselves. We arrived at Sandy Hook, and found the harbor of New York full of transports with British troops. The same day, as soon as we had dropped anchor, the Admiral hoisted signals for all the captains of the transports to come on board his ship to receive orders. In two hours they returned with orders to sail directly for Boston, as the British army had been defeated at Bunker Hill.

We weighed anchor, and set sail for Boston; arrived in three weeks, landed, and marched through the town to the *common*, where we encamped. I was soon sent on guard to Bunker Hill, where the battle had been fought. Here I saw the destruction which had been made in the loss of lives and property, and it was here that I began to have trouble and sorrow. It was nothing but hard labor; working parties engaged in building batteries every day. The weather being so much warmer than in Ireland, it overcame me, and brought on the camp distemper. I was very sick, and like to die; but he that has all power in heaven and on earth, in his hand, was pleased to spare my life through the instrumentality of the surgeon general, who visited me at the request of my worthy colonel. I soon began to get better. During my sickness I had some convictions of sin, but as soon as I got my health again, I was as

wild as ever. On the 17th of March following
Boston was evacuated, and we sailed for Halifax,
where we remained till the ensuing June. We
then received orders to embark for New York,
and had not been at sea many days when we
came up with 1200 troops from Hanover, sailed
in company with them till we came to Sandy
Hook, landed on Staten Island, and encamped
there until the 16th of August. Now, we were
32,000 strong ; 20,000 British, and 12,000 Hano-
verians. On the 17th of August we landed on
Long Island, at day-break, and marched to Bed-
ford, where the American troops lay. There I
saw the first gun that I ever saw discharged in
anger. We engaged the Americans first in a
corn-field ; had several skirmishes with them, till
we at last attacked their main body. The
foot attacked their front ; but soon after the Prince
of Wales' light horse came up, and the action became general. We took two of their generals,
and the troops they commanded, Lord Sterling
and Gen. Sullivan. In this engagement my colonel was wounded. He had two balls shot through
his body, and was taken from the field, supported
by two drummers. The American army, by this
time began to retreat, so that in the afternoon we
encamped. The second day, if I mistake not,
we understood that Gen. Washington was form-
ing his whole force to give us pitched battle at

Jamaica Plains. Twelve thousand of us were ordered to be ready at day-break. So we set off, and arrived there at night; lay all night upon our arms, and as soon as the day was dawning, we saw a horseman coming up, who informed our general that Washington was crossing the East river into New York. We were ordered to march instantly, and we ran most of the way, twelve miles. The troops in front fired and wounded some of the Americans in the boats, as they were crossing the river. We marched from Brooklyn down the river to a place called hell-gate, where the Americans had a ten gun battery, on the York side of the river. That night we built a twelve gun battery, and placed some mortars so that at day-break we were ready to lay siege to their battery. By throwing bombs and hot balls we soon blew up their magazine, and dismounted their cannon, and burned the house of the Rev. Mr. Auchmuty, where their officers lodged. The way was then clear for our army to cross the river to York Island. As soon as all the troops were crossed, the line of march was formed, and we proceeded directly for New York. We expected to have hard work to take the city, but to our surprise the enemy retreated to Haerlem Ferry, fifteen miles north-east of the city. Soon after this, we got into barracks; the American army retreated still farther into the country; our army pursued;

but as we understood the Americans did not in-
tend to meet us, if they could help it, we kept a
strong guard out to Kingsbridge, and from the
North to the East river.

During the fall, several battles were fought;
the Americans built new works at White Plains;
we sent a part of our army to Trog's Point, where
our front guard had a small engagement with
them, but nothing of much consequence till we
came to White Plains. Here we had a smart
engagement; I expected every moment to be killed, as the shot, both great and small, flew in every
direction. As soon as the action was over we
encamped for the night, and the next day, our general sent a guard and waggons to pick up the dead
and wounded. I was one of the guard, and it
caused my heart to ache to see so many of the
slain and wounded. When we picked up the
wounded and buried the dead, we struck our tents,
and marched to Dobb's Ferry, on the creek east of
Kingsbridge. Here we built an eighteen gun battery. This was in the last of October, 1776.
Next we laid siege to Fort Washington ; at three
o'clock, P. M., sent a flag of truce, and demanded
the surrender of the fort, which was accordingly
surrendered. The fort was commanded by one
Col. Magaw, an old farmer. The troops in the
fort were 2200 men. We could not keep possession of it any longer, as there were three frigates

in the North river, close to the Fort, the Phœnix, the Glasgow, and the Rose, who fired constantly against it.

When the prisoners piled their arms, they were marched a few rods from their arms, and kept under a strong guard till the next day, when they were marched to New York, and put in confinement in the sugar house, and some into the prison ships. Now winter soon came on; we were put into winter quarters; the summer had been spent in arrangements to take Philadelphia, and when it was made known to me that my colonel was to have the command in that expedition, it made me feel very bad, as I had expected whenever a vacancy should occur in his regiment to have had a commission. But I had several good friends among the officers of the army. One Capt. Nevins told me that though my colonel was gone, he would see that I should have a commission. This Capt. Nevins took the command of the regiment when my colonel went to Philadelphia. To do me kindness, Capt. Nevins made me mess-master of the regiment, to furnish the officers with dinner daily, at four o'clock. This was an easy berth; I soon became acquainted with all the officers in the regiment, and got a good deal of money; but it went as it came; I was so fond of money that I spent it freely.

CHAPTER II.

In September, 1777, my worthy friend, Capt. Nevins died suddenly, and the command was taken by one Capt. Wm. Graham. He was a good soldier, but a very profane man ; he took the command in the last of September, and in the month following, General Burgoyne was taken; when this news arrived at New York it struck a damp upon the army. I had a namesake, one Col. Burke, in another regiment, who was acquainted with our regiment, and offered me an ensign's commission. Now I thought I was going to do well; but when I went to Capt. Graham with the news, he was much offended, and told me he could not let me go, unless I enlisted two men to supply my place. It was now about the 20th of December; at this time we had a guard of 1500

men at Kingsbridge ; I was one of the number ;
we had eight redoubts with four pieces of cannon ;
these redoubts were on the east of the creek that
separates York Island from the main land.   Here
I began to think hard of getting away from the
army.   I found a Mr. Walker, a gunner, in the re-
doubt to which I was attached from the north of
Ireland.   To him I communicated the treatment
I had received from Capt. Graham, and told him
I wanted to get to Hartford if I could get away
safely.   He fell in with my plan, and as I had the
planting of the sentinels at night, I got the counter-sign.   We then made a solemn covenant that
we would be true to each other, and agreed that
we would start together the first chance we should
get.   Accordingly we set out for Col. Meigs, who
commanded Gen. Washington's leather-cap regiment of foot, on Sabbath night, the 12th of January, 1778.   The regiment which Col. Meigs commanded lay at Kings street, twenty miles from our
lines at Kingsbridge.   As we got three miles to
the West Chester bridge, we met some people of
color, going with fat turkeys to the British camp.
There were two men and two women, and they
belonged to the tories.   I had my bayonet in my
hand, and ordered them to go back, or I would run
them through.   I took one of the men by the
collar, and Walker knocked down the other.   We
then ran off almost with the speed of a horse.

We were more afraid of the tories than the British; the night was very light; the black man begged leave to walk between us; so we put him
between us, till we came to a village, where, as
the snow was deep, we were passing very near
the door of a house, when the black sprung from
us into the house, and sung out that we were going to the American army. We ran with all the
speed we had. I could then run very fast, but
Walker was a large heavy man. However I was
not going to leave him behind, for we had before
promised to be faithful to each other, and had re-
solved not to be taken alive. We soon escaped
out of the reach of the tories, and kept the main
road; but were again in danger, because there
were two regiments of British tories in the neigh-
borhood. These wore collared coats, but we
might not be able to distinguish them in the night.
I told Walker I would let no man challenge me
first. Very soon, as we were on a highland west
of Kingstreet, we saw a large party of men coming towards us. I told Walker I would challenge
them, and would know if they were Americans.
I placed Walker on my left hand, that they might
think there were more of us than there really
were. I wore a long scarlet coat, white panta-
loons, and large cocked hat, which made the officer think, as he afterwards told me, that I had a
large party with me. When they had come with-

2

in about thirty rods of us, I roared out, "who comes there?" The officer answered "friends." I ordered him to halt his party, and to advance and give the counter-sign. It was but a few minutes before he advanced, and as soon as I was convinced he was an American officer, I took off my hat, and taking my bayonet by the point, I handed it to him. He immediately sprang, clasped his arms around my body, and asked me what office I held. I told him none. He then called his party; I found him to be a lieutenant in Col. Meigs' regiment, who was himself stationed at King's street, only three miles from where we were.

The lieutenant was out on a patrole to see what he could learn of the movements of the British. He sent two or three of his men with us to the guard house, where we stayed till daylight. The colonel was then informed of us, who sent for us, to inquire what news we had brought from New York. So we told him all we knew, and what had happened to us on the road.

We found the colonel a very friendly man; he gave us all the counsel that was proper for our situation, and kept us over a great snow storm that came the next day. We then set off for West Point, to see Gen. Putnam. We found him at Fishkill; he received us very kindly; we gave him our side arms, and he made each a present of some money; here I parted with Walker, as he chose to stay in Fishkill.

Now I was like Joseph in Egypt; my mind was bent on Hartford, in Connecticut. On my way there, I put off my red coat. Gen. Putnam had given me a pass, and I had to show it every where I stopped. When I came to Hartford, I looked around some; but I wanted to see New London, as I hoped it was a large place, where I could get into some sort of business. So I came to New London, but I did not like the place; I then went ten miles into the country, to the parish of which Rev. Mr. Jewett was preacher. I there hired out to work at farming, although I knew nothing of their method of working, and had not been used to work at much hard labor.

It was now planting season, and it came very hard to me, for I knew no more what way to go to work than a Guinea negro. I soon grew tired of my work, and thought I would go to Albany; I set out, and came to Albany. Here I found Gen. Stark, and showed him my pass from Gen. Putnam. I told him I was in a strange land, with no money, and no trade, and no friends; I did not know how to labor as they do in this country, and did not know how I could support myself. The general asked if I could not go to Boston, as they wanted a man to get recruits for the Dean frigate, to form a marine company. She

was the first Letter of Marque that went to
France. I told the general I should like to set up
a fencing school, if he was willing. Some of the
officers in the American army were in town, and
wished to learn. The general gave his consent;
So I went and procured my foils, and set up a
fencing school; I did not continue it, however, but
two or three days, on account of the British
coming to Fort Stanwix.

I then went and requested a letter from the
general to the commander in chief at Boston.
So he gave me a letter to Gen. Heath, and I accordingly set out for Boston. When I got to
Worcester, it being court time, the public houses
were all so full that I could not procure a lodging.
I enquired who was the commanding officer there;
they told me his name, and I went and found him
a colonel in the army, showed him my pass from
Gen. Putnam, and told him I had a letter from
Gen. Stark to Gen. Heath, recommending me as
a military man suitable to recruit for the Dean,
Letter of Marque. The colonel treated me like a
gentleman, as he was, and gave me a note to the
last public house that had refused to take me in.
They received me there, and the next day I set
out for Boston.

CHAPTER III.

I came to Gen. Heath, showed him my pass from Gen. Putnam, and Gen. Stark's letter. He told me he would give me forty dollars per month, while he wanted me. This was about dinner time ; so the General ordered the waiter to set a a small table, and I had dinner in the same room where they dined.

After dinner, I had a warrant as a recruiting sergeant, a sword and sash, and one drummer and fifer to attend me. I kept on recruiting till I enlisted the number they wanted. But before I got through, they began to offer me a commission. I told them I was willing to do all I could to help

2*

them, but that I could not join the army, because
if I did, and should be taken by the British, I
should suffer death.   Therefore they did not insist
upon it.

When the company which I had recruited was
full, Gen. Hancock ordered me to drill the company two hours in the morning, and two hours at
night, which I did, and in three or four weeks,
they were fit for action.   The day was set for
Gen. Hancock to come on board the ship, and see
the men go through the manual exercise.   The
company had a captain and two lieutenants; they
were paraded on the quarter deck; the officers
took their places, and I did mine, but these gentlemen knew no more how to put their company
through the manual exercise than children.   Gen.
Hancock knew so, and he ordered me to carry the
company through the exercise.   I stepped out in
front of the company, drew my sword and carried
the company through the exercise without the
least mistake.   The General then thanked the
company for their good behavior, and thanked me
also.   Then he told me to dismiss the company,
and to go to the purser of the ship, and get four
gallons of spirits, and treat the company.

There was a French lieutenant on board the
ship, a proud, haughty fellow, who could not bear
to see what notice the general officers took of me.
As I was walking the quarter deck one afternoon,

he ordered me off in something of a passion. I
told him I thought I had a right to walk there ; he
then swore, and cursed me as an English rascal,
and ordered one of the boatswains of the ship to
put me in irons. The boatswain put a pair of
irons on my hands. This threw me into a great
passion ; I called for pen and ink, and sent the
lieutenant a challenge, telling him to lay down his
commission, and I would show him British play ;
but he would not accept of it. The company then
threatened to throw him overboard. Capt. Samuel Nicholson, who commanded the ship, then
took me on shore, to prevent disturbance, and so
the thing was dropped.

The officers now all wished me to accept of a
commission; but I would not for fear of being
taken. I then took leave of them, and went to
New London, and began to live with a Mr. Darrow to learn the trade of making nails. I was to
work for him eighteen months for what I could
learn, and he was to board me. When I had
lived with him one year, I could make as many
nails as he could. I was then very active. I
made 60,000 lath nails while I lived with him for
Mr. David Trumbull.

After my time was out, I worked for wages ;
so now I began to get clothes, and to form acquaintances with the people. I also began to go to
meeting, to hear Mr. Jewett, of the north parish

in New London, who was called a good preacher,
Soon after this, the two deacons, Otis and Chester
by name, invited me to come to their houses,
which I did, and they always gave me the best of
counsel.   By this time, I had seen the wickedness of the Roman Catholic clergy, and was ra·
tionally convinced that God only could forgive
sins.   Sometimes I thought I took a good deal of
pleasure in the company of these good men.

I worked in the summer season for both these
men, and found them to be godly men indeed, and
though I did not love religion, I thought they had
something which I had not; I pleased them, and
went to meeting with them and their families,
though I went more to be seen of men than to get
good.   At this time I was looked upon as a steady
young man; I was well clothed, and went into
the best of company.   The young people used to
dance, and as they knew little about it, when they
met, I used to be their teacher.   I soon got the
good will of the young people, and I can safely
say, that I was as well beloved as in my own
country.

CHAPTER IV.

His marriage. Removal to Colchester. Is cheated by one
of his countrymen. Charged with being a spy, and put
in irons. His release. Goes to Tyringham, Mass. Is
defrauded, and accused of being a deserter from the American army, and thrown into prison. His rescue, and return
to New London.

By this time the old people began to tell me to
get married, as they wanted me to settle among
them, and as my trade was then good, I soon after
married a young woman named Lettice Maynard,
who lived with John Dolbear, Esq., in the north
parish of New London; I was married the 15th of
April, 1780, by the Rev. Mr. Jewett, of the same
parish. I continued to work for my old employer, Mr. Darrow, and as soon as my wife was
ready to remove, he furnished a house for us to
live in near the shop.

Now things seemed to go on favorable for some
time, until Whig and Tory business came on. I

then removed to Colchester, and went to work at my trade. Not long after, I went to New London, to see Col. Harris, two miles out of town; but as I was going through New London, I found one of my countrymen there in jail; he requested me to get him out; he needed about sixty dollars, which he owed at a boarding house, and had nothing to pay the debt; I paid the money, and took him out, and he agreed to go home with me, and work out the debt. We went to Col. Harris', and stayed till late in the evening. I had a hired horse, belonging to Josiah Foot, of Colchester. The man stepped to the door, took the horse, saddle and bridle, and some goods I had in the saddle bags, and rode off. The next day I advertised him, and he was soon brought back by one Frink, a butcher who lived in New London. This butcher and the runaway told the authority when they came back, that I was a spy from the British army, and ought to be hung; for they had seen my commission one day, in New London. I had gone home to Colchester, but the authority sent and brought me to New London, where I was examined before Col. Ledyard, who commanded at New London.

I was then sent to Fort Trumbull, and my hands put in irons. I sent to Colchester, to Col. Eliphalet Bulkley, who was in partnership with me in the nail business, and he told Col. Ledyard that the whole story about my being a spy was false; so I was let go, and returned to Colchester, and went to work again. But if it had not been for Col. Bulkley, I might have been hanged for a spy. But the glorious God had something to do for me, although I could not see it then. This was in September, 1782, and the next spring I went back to live in the north parish of New London. My employer and his father were both what were called tories; therefore I must be one too. This caused me a good deal of uneasiness, but I tried to keep as still as I could, and had nothing to do with either of the parties. Soon after this they wanted me to go into the three years service. I told them if I was ever so willing, Congress had passed an act not to enlist foreigners, and finally, to get rid of them, I went to the town of Tyringham, in Massachusetts, and worked there six months for a Mr. Chapin. He was to give me six and thirty pounds worth in land and provisions in the fall, and I did so much work. I served him faithfully, but when my time was out he contrived to get rid of paying me by telling the commanding officer there that I was a deserter from the American army. He got himself deputized, and took me with a warrant, and he and two of his sons pinioned my hands behind my back, and carried me to Great Barrington jail. There I was thirty days, when Aaron Kellogg and his wife, of Colchester, came to Great Barrington to visit Gen. Fellows. Mrs. Kellogg was a good friend of mine, and when she heard that there was a man in jail who used to live in Colchester, she came to see me. When I told her the reason of my being there, and how Mr. Chapin had used me, she told me she would have me out before night if it cost her horse and carriage, and she was as good as her word.

She and her husband, and Gen. Fellows came to see me, and heard me tell over the whole story. The general, like a gentleman and a Christian, treated me kindly, and gave me a written pass to go home to my wife and child. I then set off for Chapin, and when he saw me coming he was much surprised, and asked me how I got out of jail. I told him I proved to Gen. Fellows that I was not a deserter from Washington's army, as he had charged me with being, and told him further that I wanted my pay. But he made such bills of cost against me that I had not more than forty shillings coming. I then took my leave of him, and set off for New London.

CHAPTER V.

Hears of the burning of New London; repairs to the same.
Falls into bad company, and the habit of excessive drinking. Reproved by pious friends. Falls into a snow drift
in a fit of intoxication, and comes near perishing. A master put over him. Leaves the place in anger. Goes
across Connecticut river to Northford, in Branford. His
intemperance increases. Becomes alarmed at his guilt,
and resolves to cease from hard drinking.

By the time I got to Hartford, I heard that Gen.
Arnold had burnt New London. I stopped quick
when I heard this news, for I thought I could help
some if I was there. I soon came where Mrs.
Burke was, but stayed there only one night, for
the militia were then called out, and I volunteered
myself, and went to Fort Griswold, where Col.
Ledyard was killed. It was a shocking sight to
see so many killed at their own doors, as it were.
As I was a military man, I insisted on helping
all I could. I stayed one week, and then came

3

home ; and soon after I went to work at my trade
for a Mr. Hartley, of New London.

Here I got into bad company, and took to drinking. This conduct opened a door for all evil. I
now kept moving from one part of the country to
another, till we had four children. In the spring
of 1789, I worked for a Mr. Herrick, at Norwich
Landing. He was a Baptist deacon, and used to
have meetings at his own house. Here I had
some convictions by reason of the preaching that
I heard. I began to think of dying, and how bad
I had acted. My wife would often talk to me for
my drinking, and for swearing, which I was sometimes guilty of. Deacons Otis and Chester, used
also to reprove me, sometimes very sharply, for by
this time I had got to be a town talk.

I lived near deacon Otis, and got out of clothes,
and spent all my time in drinking rum or cider,
which would make me as drunk as if I drank
spirits. I went to New London once in the month
of January, and on my return, when I got within
twenty rods of home, I was so overcome with
liquor that I fell into a snow drift, at ten o'clock at
night. Here I should have froze to death, if the
Lord had not sent my next neighbor that way.
He had lost his team, and was looking for them.
When he found me, he thought I was dead ; but
he took me up, and carried me in his arms to the
house where my wife and children were. They

rubbed my limbs, and brought me to. Soon after this, Judge Hillhouse put a deacon Rogers a master over me. I could not bear this treatment; although I would now hold up both hands to have a master put over any man that should conduct as I did then, and I will have reason to bless God to all eternity that the worthy Hillhouse put a master over me when he did, alhough I did not think so then.

When I heard that I had a master put over me, I asked his name. They told me that it was deacon Jabez Rogers, a Baptist. I took a stick in my hand, and went to his house to whip him, but he was not at home; and I have often blessed the Lord since, that the deacon was gone from home, for I might have killed him, although he was not to blame. I came home, and told my wife that I would leave the town. So I picked up my tools, for as to clothes I had not two dollars worth in the world. I was at this time, on a level with the brute creation, without any fear of God or man before my eyes. I told my wife I would go and live and work somewhere else, for I would not stay any longer among such bad people. She told me she never wished to see me any more unless I became a new creature; and she never did see me after that, till, as I hope, both she and myself became new creatures.

I now started, and crossed Connecticut river,

and went to Branford, to the parish of Northford, ten miles east of New Haven, I got there the 14th of April, 1788. Here I went to work for a Mr. Joseph Rogers, who was a great drunkard, and Joel, his brother, also. This was company that suited me. So I went to work, and Mr. Rogers and Col. Drake of New Haven, said they thought they never saw better nails that came from England. Now I got my name up as a good nailor, as I was. But when my month was out, I must have a drunken frolic.

Mr. Rogers had a brother-in-law, one Mr. Baldwin, who kept a public house, and was captain of the militia company ; so Mr. Rogers took me with him to Capt. Baldwin's, to training, where he and I had high times, as we called it. The next day I was not fit to work. So I went eight or ten miles to North Branford, and stopped at the house of a Capt. Foot. His wife was a gay woman, and gave me something to drink. She liked to hear me sing, for I was then a mighty singer at common singing. From this place I went on, until I came to the old town of Branford, where I staid till the next Sabbath day. When I heard people say it was the Sabbath, I felt guilty to be among strangers on the Lord's day, and drunk at the same time.

So I finally shut myself up in a room with one John Baldwin, until night. This is the only night I ever passed when I could not tell where I slept. I had been so drunk all the week before, that I had lost the time. I must have slept in Baldwin's barn. The next morning, before sun-rise, I found myself in the road that led to Rogers', where I had worked. I came to a brook of water, and washed me, and wiped myself with a rag of a handkerchief that I had with me.

By this time the sun was just rising. The morning was beautiful, and all creation seemed to be praising God but drunken Burke. All at once, such a shock of trembling seized me that every joint in my body shook. I was like Belshazzer when the hand wrote on the wall of his palace. I was struck under such conviction of my sin and wickedness that I thought God would be just if he should crush my body and soul into hell in a moment. I dare not ask for mercy, for it was a settled point with me that hell must be my por-tion to all eternity. I did not know what to do; As for going back to Rogers', I thought if I did, every one that looked me in the face would read my character. My conscience flew in my face, and told me that I must perish if I did not repent of my sins.

O my friends, if the damned in hell feel any greater horror than I did, it is because their tor-ment is greater; but how can they endure any

3*

greater torment than mine was on the 19th day of May, 1773.

Here I looked back upon my sin and wickedness, a poor creature that had broken the laws of God in ten thousand instances. Now I thought of deacons Otis and Chester's good counsel; and then of my poor wife, and the thoughts brought a hell into my soul. Especially the thoughts of how I had misused my wife and children. By this time I had arrived at Rogers', in Northford. He had got a hogshead of rum of Col. Drake, which he had paid for in nails; so he was glad to see me come back, and went and made a bowl of punch, and asked me to drink. I told him I was willing to go to work for him, but I hoped he would not see me drink any more rum, if I lived with him ten years. Then he laughed at me, and told me I had only been having a drunken frolic, I had got scared.

So we made another bargain. The agreement was drawn up by Esq. Clark, of Northford. I was to work six months, and Rogers was to let me have a cow in the fall, and the rest in nails and money. I went to work, but felt the greatest distress in my mind. I worked in the shop alone. On the 22d of May, of a Thursday morning, I went to the shop to work at day-break, and all at once, it seemed as though I was called by name, William, you must repent, or else you will perish forever. Here, for the first time, I kneeled down in earnest prayer for mercy, and made a solemn covenant promise with my God, that if his holy majesty would give me strength to keep it, I never would drink another drop of spirit, or even cider, or any thing by which I might be led to offend.

CHAPTER VI.

His conversion. Return to his family. Interview with Lieut. Chapman. With the Rev. Mr. Cook.

I then endeavored to give myself to God, and to my poor wife and little ones. I was soon after called to breakfast, but could not eat any thing. By this time the neighbors thought I was going to be crazy, and asked me what ailed me. I told them I had been mad all my days until now; but I hoped the Lord had now been pleased to bring me to myself. I kept at work till Saturday night. The next morning, the Lord's day, the happiest day I had ever seen, I got up—for during the past week I had not slept as much as one night's sleep till that night; but in the morning, I found an old Bible, belonging to Mr. Roger's mother, a good woman, though I did not know of it till after this day.

I went out about sunrise, to a mountain three fourths of a mile east of Northford meeting-house, where I spent the day. I did not dare to go to meeting for fear I should disturb the congregation. So I went to the mountain, and read and cried all day alone; but I could find nothing in the Bible but what seemed like artillery of cannon levelled at my poor soul. When the day was spent, so that the sun was not more than a quarter of an hour high, I began to think I was beyond the reach of mercy. I set off for home—home I had none. I had to go through a piece of corn, of about one acre, with a beautiful apple-tree standing in the middle of it. The sun was now setting. I said to myself, may be this is the happy spot where the Lord will hear me. I kneeled down with the Bible open in my hand. I laid it down open before me, and made a resolution never to get up until I found mercy. I spoke aloud. If I perished, I would perish here, *begging for mercy.*

Here I was from sunset till the church bell rang at nine o'clock, crying for mercy for Christ's sake. Soon after the bell had done ringing, all at once, as though the words were spoken by White-field in the pulpit, I thought I heard these words— " I say unto you that likewise joy shall be in heaven, over one sinner that repenteth more than over ninety and nine just persons which need no repent. ance." My distress and burden left me in a moment, and such light and love to God and men as was let into my heart and soul, all earth and hell

never since could put out. I went to Mr. Rogers'
rejoicing, and calling on all Christians to bless
and praise God for what he had done for my poor
soul.

Soon after I came in, they began to ask where
I had been; I told them I had been on the moun-,
tain, I asked their forgiveness for my wicked
conduct. They all said I had behaved well since
I had lived there; but I told them I had been left
to serve the devil for ten years past, and now I
meant to serve God. Then the old lady, Mr.
Rogers' mother, began to talk to me, and to rejoice with me. She thought I would be crazy;
but I told her, as the apostle Paul told the king—
"I now speak forth the words of truth and sober-
ness." I talked with Mr. Rogers and his brother
Joel, and told them they must perish unless
they repented; and I was bound to tell them so, if
they put me out of the house for it. I could tell
them, although it was late, I could say as Manas-
seh, that this night *drunken Burke* could say that
the Lord, He is God. They all wept, and we
never went to bed until break of day.

> " Oh, if I had an angel's voice,
> And could be heard from pole to pole,
> I would to all the listening world,
> Proclaim thy goodness to my soul."

The next day, some good people came to see

me, and lent me some good books. I visited these Christian people at their houses, and went also to see a young candidate that was preaching at Northford, where their minister was dead. This young man was Mr. Hale, who was afterwards settled in Lisbon, east of Norwich, and a lovely young man he was. I used to go to visit him every evening, as he boarded in the next house to me. O, the happy hours I have spent in his company. And when I used to go to my work in the morning, I would long for the evening to come again, that I might go and converse with Mr. Hale.

I now began to hear the sound of the glorious gospel of Christ, that I had so long despised. As soon as my time was out, I got my pay of Mr. Rogers, and set out to see my family. I had before sent my wife a letter containing the happy news concerning me; but she had also obtained a hope in Christ before my letter arrived, and I have every reason to believe that she did meet with a saving change while I was absent from her. We had a joyful meeting. Deacon Otis came to see me, and other neighbors. The good man, deacon Otis, and also deacon Rogers, the man whom Judge Hillhouse had put master over me, both prayed with us.

Now I had many crooks to straighten. I had once challenged Lieut. Chapman, of New London, but happily he refused to meet me. I now went to his house, to settle with him, but he had gone to Judge Hillhouse's. It was a very rainy day; I went to meet him, and when I saw him coming towards me, I dropped on my knees in the mud, and asked his forgiveness. He said he could forgive me, as he knew that liquor was the cause of my abuse of him. I felt much better when this business was settled.

I got some tools this fall, and went to work for myself. The neighbors found me stock. The next spring, the good man deacon Otis, and others, helped to build me a small house and shop, so that I had a place of my own. The Baptists now wanted to have me join their church. I told them I was waiting God's time for direction, and that I should not join any church at present. I went at this time to hear a Mr. Palmer, a Baptist preacher, because I was six miles from the Rev. Mr. Cook, of Montville.

As soon as the spring came on, I went to see Mr. Cook. He had not heard any thing about the change I had met with. When I went to his house he was in the field at work, and when he saw me coming, and remembered my former life, he would have nothing to say to me; but I told him if he would not go home and converse with me, my heart was so full that it would burst. So he went to his house, and I told him what the

4

Lord had done for my soul. I also asked him whether one who was baptized in infancy ought to be baptized again. He answered no. I told him all my father's children were baptized in their infancy by the Roman Catholic clergy. I then told him how the Baptists wanted me to join their church; but I told him that I did not think a holy God ever called any to preach the gospel unless they were qualified for the work, both by the letter and the spirit, and those preachers in Colchester were not so.

The good man then read several passages of scripture to me, and explained them. He asked me to come and see him again. As he had not heard that I had become serious, I referred him to deacon Otis. He smiled, and said he believed I was quite altered since he saw me last. He lent me the "Guide to Christ," and I read it with much pleasure. After this, I was a constant attendant on his preaching while I lived in his parish. He was the minister after the Rev. Mr. Jewett.

CHAPTER VII.

Soon after this visit to Mr. Cook, I went to see
Timothy Green, Esq., of New London, at his in-
vitation, and he gave me the life of Col. Gardiner. He told me he rejoiced much, as I was the
last man in the world that he should have expected to see looking for mercy. He kindly offered
to take one of my boys to help me, as I had four
children. I soon after carried my eldest son, and
left him with Mr. Green, to learn to be a printer.

At this time, I found a book in his son's book-
store called Thomas Boston. I took a liking to
the book, and asked the price. He told me five
shillings. I had not got the money then, but he

told me I might take the book, and pay him when I could. So I took it and came home. Now I thought I was well off for books. But I had no Bible, only a Testament that belonged to my wife. So I went to Norwich and bought a Bible, and paid for it in nails. I put God's own book into my bosom, between my shirt and waistcoat. When I rode across Norwich bridge it was dark; it was in November. I looked up to heaven, for it was the first time that I had crossed that bridge sober. I came home rejoicing that God had given me the Bible. O what a soul feast I used to have in reading my Bible, and those other good books.

Soon after this, the brethren of the church told me I ought to join the church, for they had charity for me. I used to tell them I was waiting God's time. I wanted to satisfy myself for fear I might be deceived. So I went to see Mr. Cook several times. One time as he was conversing with me about joining the church, I told him I had a confession to make whenever I joined the church. He told me he did not know of any confession which I ought to make. I told him I looked upon myself to stand in relation to God and his people by my baptism; and that I ought to make a public confession of the sin and wickedness that I had publicly committed. Mr. Cook told me that he generally wrote a confes-

sion and read it publicly; but I told him that I
never should feel right until I had made a public
confession with my own lips.

When the time was come that I was to join
the church, I lived six miles from the meeting.
So I got a horse of one of my neighbors, for myself and wife to ride to meeting. When Mr.
Cook took his text I thought I should have fainted
away. The text was Joshua vii. 19th and 20th
verses. "And Joshua said unto Achan—my son,
give, I pray thee, glory to the Lord God of Israel,
and make confession unto him; and tell me now
what thou hast done; hide it not from me. And
Achan answered Joshua and said—Indeed, I have
sinned against the Lord God of Israel, and thus
and thus have I done." When he had done his
sermon he told the congregation my request, and
then he told me the church was ready to hear
what I had to say. I went into the broad isle, and
looking up to God, I begged the divine forgiveness,
and that also of the church and congregation, for
my sin and wickedness, and for setting such a bad
example before the dear youth of the parish.
The church was very crowded. The people had
heard that drunken Burke was going to join the
church, and make a public confession, and they
came from all quarters. There was not a joint in
my body but that trembled, and I can safely say
there was not one present, young or old, but that

4*

wept. And O the joy and satisfaction there was in my heart and soul. I felt like a young prince just come in the possession of a crown.

> " When God revealed his gracious name,
> And changed my mournful state,
> My rapture seemed a pleasing dream,
> The grace appeared so great.
>
> The world beheld the glorious change,
> And did Thy power confess;
> My tongue broke out in unknown strains,
> And sang surprising grace."

O, the happy days I spent with this church during the three years that I continued to live in Montville. After this I removed to Colchester, where I bought a small place, and where my trade was better than at Montville. But here I had many trials. One was about the half way covenant. I told them there was no half way heaven, and no half way hell. But it must be altogether, eternal happiness, or eternal misery with man in the other world.

I had another trial with a drunken man, who used to tell me that I had got proud, and would not drink rum with him, but would drink *wine*. Once this man met me in the street. " Fight," said he, " you Irish devil," and struck me on the breast. I ran away from him, but he came up with me again, and took a quid of tobacco out of his mouth, and struck it into mine, so that it made me gag for some minutes. And again he said, "Fight, you devil." "Mr. Cone," I replied, "I fear fighting no more now than I ever did, but I fear sinning." So I ran off and left him. The next morning I was going up street with some nails to Capt. Hubbard's store, and met the three select men. I told them how Cone treated me the last night, and they told him he must be civil or else they would put a master over him. After that he never abused me.

I now built me a large shop, took two boys to learn my trade, and hired two journeymen, and got a good living. Gen. Champion, of East Haddam, furnished me with stock; and now in three years, I had a house and barn, and thirty acres of land, in the town street of Colchester, that cost me £200. But Gen. Champion wished me to come and live at East Haddam, so as to save carting the nail rods so far. I soon after sold my place in Colchester, and removed to East Haddam. Before I removed to Colchester, I used to get a minister to preach a sermon annually, on the 25th of May, in commemoration of the day when I met with my change, and I continued to have this done till I began to travel.

After I got through with Gen. Champion, I went to work for Cowles and Meigs, of Middletown. I made a contract with them, by which they were

to furnish me as many rods as I should find workmen for. I was to make 8, 10, and 20 penny
nails; put them up in good casks, for which they
were to pay, delivered at Gen. Champion's store.
As soon as this contract was done, I made a de-
mand for two tons of nail rods. I kept at work
in this way until I had got seventy-five acres of
land, and a new house, in East Haddam, Millington Society, where Rev. Dr. William Lyman
preached. Now things seemed to go well with
me until Mr. Meigs broke. By reason of his fail-
ure I was obliged to sell my place. My wife was
weakly, so I was obliged to buy all my bedding,
and my children's clothes; and now here I was,
stript of all I had, and left where the Lord found
me on Branford mountain.

Here I was left with a weakly woman, who
for the last three years that I lived in Colchester,
and ever since, had been unable to take care of
herself. We had ten children. I had not the
value of a bushel of corn left, and my own
health was now poor by reason of hard work and
great trouble.

CHAPTER VIII.

This was in August, 1801. I hired a small
house for the coming winter, and was constantly crying at the throne of grace that God would
grant me wherewithal to support my family. In
the spring of 1802 I went to Montville, and the
church there helped me to some provisions. Before these were gone, Capt. Sylvanus Tinker, of
East Haddam sent for me to come and see him.
He was a merchant, and I had received a great
many favors of him before I sold my place. He
thought it would be best to sell the place at auc-
tion, and we tried to do so, but the people were
not willing to give half its value.   So Capt. Tinker, who was at the vendue, told the people that

he would keep me on the place as long as he thought best. So it was sold at private sale.

Sometime in the coming fall, a friendly doctor from New London called on me, and asked me to come and see him. So I went to his house, and he undertook to prescribe for my health. He used to give me medicine, and also to take me out to ride every pleasant morning. I had not been with him more than a week before I was much better in health.

By this time he and Dr. Thompson wished me to go and ride for them. They thought it would help my health. They were apothecaries, and had a great deal of money due to them at Albany, New York, and Boston, and all through the country. I asked them what my family would do while I was gone. They said they would take care of my family. So I went for them to Boston; thence to Albany. By the time I had got to Boston, I felt much better, and the more I rode, the better I felt. From Albany I went to Hudson, and from thence to Kinderhook flats, on the east side of the North river. Here I found that man of God, the Rev. John B. Romeyn, now Rev. Dr. Romeyn, of New York. Here I had a soul feast with him and his people. I spent the Sabbath with him, and communed with his church.

Monday, took my leave of him, and started for

New York. From New York I went to Philadelphia. When had performed my business there, I returned to New London with pretty good health. The doctor set me out again ; I brought him in some money and goods. My family was well taken care of, and I continued riding in this way for about six months.

The doctor then sent me out with a pair of horses, and a covered waggon, and $10,000 worth of medicine, and receipts for medicine that was out on commission. He also sent a young man with me to drive the waggon, and take care of the horses. I travelled on this route 1825 miles by a written journal. I sold all out, and collected a great many hundred dollars for the doctor. I returned, August 1803, and settled with him, and gave good satisfaction.

I had now money enough to provide for my family against the coming winter. Besides, on these journeys I formed a great many Christian acquaintances. I also got an extensive acquaintance with the country. But I little thought at this time, that the Lord was preparing me to distribute his blessed word.

Col. Green, of New London, was a printer, and he now employed me to go through the state, to procure subscribers for the works of the Rev. John Newton, in nine volumes. He agreed to give me fifteen shillings a day, and to bear my

own expenses; so I started. The people were
pleased to see me trying to get that good man's
works printed once more, and the clergy were every where ready to befriend me. They said they
had rather see me engaged in that business than
in selling medicine. I returned to New London
in November, 1802.

Soon after this, there began to be a revival of
religion, in Boston, or rather in Charlestown, near
to Boston. Col. Green then wished me to go
there to get subscribers to Newton's works. This
was in December; it was very cold weather. Col.
Green asked me how I would go. I told him I
would go as I had been through this state. But
he told me no; he would give me $20, and I
might go to Boston, be as prudent as I could, and
stay till the $20 were gone. Then if I got 400
subscribers he would give me $10 on the hundred.
If not, I should lose my time, and he would lose
his money. I thought it was a hard bargain, but
I was like to be out of all business. This was at
his house, at tea. I asked him when I should set
out. He said, "to-morrow morning." I told
him I would give him an answer in the morning.

My heart ached—for I had a son at home very
sick; and to be at home myself, and nothing coming, was very discouraging. So after tea, I went
into his garden, and it being very dark, I got into
a place which was very private, and poured out

my soul unto God that he would direct me to that which would be best. When I got through prayer, I had such an impression on my mind that I did not doubt but that it would be best for me to go. So in the morning I told Col. Green I would, but that I must go home and see my wife and sick son before I went, and that I would then start in two days.

I came home and found my son some better. I asked him and my wife if they were willing to have me go. They thought it would be best that I should go. So I set off for Boston, which I knew to be a dear place for man and horse to live in. But my Christian friends sent many letters by me to make me friends. One of which was a letter from Gov. Jonathan Trumbull, of Lebanon. I had also a letter from Rev. Dr. Lyman, of Millington, to Rev. Dr. Morse, of Charlestown, which I gave to the Doctor, and communed with him concerning all my trials. Dr. Morse also gave me the names of several gentlemen for me to call on. I went on every day, I hope faithfully for my employer.

I called on the Rev. William Ellery Channing, and gave him a letter from his uncle, the Rev. Henry Channing, of New London. As soon as he had read it, he said he was happy to see me, and gave me a number of gentlemen's names to call on—one of which was Mr. Samuel H. Walley, the son-in-law of Gov. Philips. By the time I came to Mr. Walley's house, he had heard of my misfortunes, and that I had a weakly wife.

When I came to his house, it was a snowy and very disagreeable day to be out; but I took that advantage in order to find gentlemen at home. As soon as I rapped at the door, he came and opened it himself. I felt tender to be disturbing great men on such a stormy day. So I made some apology for disturbing him. I asked him if Mr. Walley lived there. He said his name was Walley; so I told him my name was Burke, from Connecticut. He took me by the hand, and bade me welcome to his house. He said he had heard of me, and wished to see me. He very kindly asked me how my sick family was when I came away. I was surprised at these questions, but found that my friends had told him the condition of my family, and my misfortunes in their letters.

He asked to look at my subscription paper. I showed it to him, and he subscribed for six copies of Newton's works, and then put his hand into his desk, and gave me $20, and told me he would see me again in a few days. I thanked him, and took my leave, and when I got into the street I longed to find a private place, where I might thank my heavenly Father for his goodness and mercy to me in my low estate. I hope I praised the Lord for his goodness to my body and soul.

In a few days I was astonished to see how many invited me to their houses to eat and lodge with them. If I had been in Boston seven years, I could not have thought to have had more friends.

I used to go to meeting every night, and had happy times to see so many living Christians. They soon began to call on me to pray in their meetings, because Dr. Morse had told them of my remarkable change. Sometimes I used to go to hear the Baptists. They seemed to be very kind, and made me some presents. They requested me to tell my experience in hopes that it would be the means of doing good. So, whenever I told it, I related it in its true color, and it made them weep bitterly. I had poor success in getting subscribers, because the printers in Boston said that Green was poor printer.

CHAPTER IX.

One day I met Mr. Channing, and he told me he was glad to see me, and wished me to go to his house. So I went, and he told me I must come to his house again the next day, and go with him to Mr. Walley's to take dinner. I felt tender about going, as I was poorly clothed; but he said that Mr. Walley told him he must bring me with him. Little did I know what the Lord was working for the good of my body and soul. So the next day at two o'clock Mr. Channing and I went to Mr. Walley's. There we found Gov. Phillips and his wife, and some other ladies and gentlemen that I did not know. I was introduced to Gov. Phillips and his lady. While we sat at dinner, the Governor asked me what I thought of dancing. I

5*

was surprised that so great a character and so pious
a man should ask me such a question. So I dropped my knife and fork, and asked the Governor if
he meant people of the world or professors of religion. He said—*professors.* I told his honor I
had no opinion of my own to offer; but "if your
honor will turn to the 21st chapter of the book of
Job, 11, 12, 13, and 14th verses, there you will find
an answer to the question." I told him that dancing, simply considered, was no hurt, but the consequence that followed it was that John the Baptist lost his head in the prison, because the dancing of the daughter of Herodius pleased the wicked old Monarch. Mr. Channing then asked me
if David did not dance. I told him I did not
understand the original language of the Bible, but
that David was so pleased to see the ark of God
come home to its place, that he rejoiced, stepping
quick, and skipping about, and they called it dancing in the English language. But let it be called
what it might, I would to God that all Boston were
dancing with the spirit that David had, that day,
and I would leave this honorable company and go
into the street and dance with them. So the company at the table clapped their hands.

When dinner was over, I told Mr. Walley that
I must be excused, as I was a hireling, and must
be going to attend to my employer's business. So
I went into the hall where my loose coat was, and

Mr. Walley was going to wait on me, but the Governor put his son-in-law back, and helped me to put on my loose coat himself. Then he took me by the hand, and said he hoped to see me at his own house in a few days, and then handed me ten dollars. I thanked his honor, and then went· to get subscribers. I was very busy, but could not get the number that Col. Green wished. I had many invitations to visit my friends in Boston; and one day the Governor sent his only son, Mr. Jonathan Phillips, to invite me to dine with him; and I went accordingly, and was treated more like a brother than a stranger. O my dear reader, how little I felt in my own eyes, a poor stranger treated so by God's dear children; and in this way my acquaintance began with Gov. Phillips;—and blessed be God, that acquaintance continues to this day.

Now I took my leave of my friends in Boston, and set out for home. When I had mounted my horse to go to Boston, he had nothing on his back but myself and saddle bags; and now on my return the Lord was pleased to load me down with money and clothing for my poor wife and children.

So when I came to New London, I called on Mr. Green, and gave him all the subscribers' names I had got, but they were so few he never printed the work. When I arrived at home and my wife had seen all the Lord had done for us, we had a thanksgiving day of it.

I found my son that I had left sick much better, and he soon got quite well. In the following spring, a man from New York called on me, and said he was directed to me to collect a debt of $70 for him, and as money was scarce, he said he would take cattle for the debt. So I went to the debtor, and he paid me in cattle. I sold the cattle for money, and sent it to the man by the Post that rode from Hartford to Hudson. This job afforded me some help. The following May I went to Boston, and my friend Mr. Walley proposed to me that if I would get a stand in a good place, my friends in Boston would advance me $500 in money and goods, that I might open a small store. I thanked them for their offer, and accepted of it; and then came home and set up a small store in Hebron, ten miles from Millington. But I could do nothing there, because my orders were to keep the goods rather than to sell them on credit.

So I went to New London, called on my friend, the Rev. Henry Channing, and spent the night with him. The next morning he took me and introduced me to Gen. Huntington, and told him all about me. The General was glad to see me, and told me he would be glad to have me come to New London. So I went to Col. Green, who had a store with $1200 worth of groceries and books in

it. He said if I would take charge of them, I
might remove there as soon as I pleased. So I
removed to New London, where I staid some
time. Here I enjoyed myself very much in the
society of Christians. Here I began my acquaintance with that most heavenly man, Gen. Jededi-
ah Huntington. He was a real friend to me till
the day of his death. Many happy hours have
we spent with each other, talking about our Father's house, eternal in the heavens. During the
time that I lived in New London, the General
used to come very often to see Mrs. Burke and our
dear children; and when we wanted any thing,
and had not the money, he would advance me
what I wanted.

After this I removed back to East Haddam,
Millington Society, and traded there about two
years. Here I could not sell goods for the cash,
and I began to feel uneasy for fear I should not
get money enough to pay for the goods. So I
went to Boston, and told my feelings to my friends.
At the same time I carried a hundred dollars in
silver to Mr. Walley. He told me that I need
not be concerned for I should not be hurt. Soon
after this, he (Mr. W.) sent me a letter, to have
me pay for some groceries that I owed him for in
New London. I went to carry the pay to the men
that I owed, which pay was in goods. I set out
for New London the 7th day of December, 1807,

on horseback, and had a man, and waggon, and
horses with me to carry the goods.   The distance
to New London was twenty miles; and when we
got to the ten mile stone, my horse stumbled and
pitched me among the stones that lay by the side
of the road.   The horse fell on my left leg, and
was rolling back and forth till my leg was broken
in several pieces—my collar bone was put out, and
my body much bruised.   While I was under the
horse, I expected every moment to be crushed to
death, but mercy spared me.   As a holy God was
pleased to order it, I fell near a school house, and
two boys came to help me.   By this time the
horse had got off from my leg, and I told the boys
to call the man in the waggon, and tell him my
leg was broke.   Mr. Otis, the man who drove the
waggon, came, and carried me in his arms and put
me in the waggon, and carried me to New London, where I was thirty-one days before I could go
across the room with crutches.

Here, in this fiery trial, I had some of the happiest days I had ever enjoyed.   I had all the godly
round me every day, and the man of God, General
Huntington.   He had sent for Dr. Sweet, the
great bone-setter, and had paid him $10 for set-
ting my limbs.   Here I saw more of the goodness
of God in disposing my friends to be so kind to me,
a poor unworthy creature.   Shortly after this I
wrote to Gov. Phillips, and to his son, Walley,—

and the next mail stage brought me $77, which they sent to defray the expenses of my sickness. Here I could see again how the gold and silver on earth is the Lord's, and that He can incline the hearts of them that have it to supply the wants of his needy children that put their trust in Him. O that men would praise the Lord for his goodness and mercy. On the 8th day of January my friends sent me home to my family. They sent a hack-coach and a very steady driver, and a second man to take care of me in the carriage. We arrived at my house about sunset, where my wife and children, and all my friends were glad to see me. I was confined to my house until spring, when I rode to New London, and got Col. Green to print 3500 small sermons. I was able to ride a gentle horse, and to distribute these sermons in the neighboring towns.

CHAPTER X.

In June, 1808, I received a letter from a Christian friend in the island of Nantucket, where the
Rev. Mr. Gurney preached. They had a great
revival, and promised to pay all my expenses going and coming, if I would visit them. So I took
a number of tracts, and shipped on board the sloop
Julia, Capt. William Spencer, a fine young man;
nothing wanting to him but grace. As soon as I
got on board, I told the captain I wanted the privilege, when the weather would permit, to call the
crew together, to read and pray with them. The
captain said he should be happy to have me do so.
We arrived safely at Nantucket, and I was received by Mr. Dickinson, and the Rev. Mr. Gurney,
since dead. I staid with them till the first of

6

August, and had heavenly times of it. **The**
church and people were very loath to have me go
away. Squire Hussey offered to support me while
I lived if I would remain with them. He was an
Attorney and very rich. I thanked him, but told
him I must go home. So the night before I came
away there was a full meeting, and before the blessing was pronounced, Mr. Gurney told the people
that their dear brother Burke was poor in this
world's goods, but he hoped rich in faith; that he
was now returning to his family, and he Mr.
Gurney, trusted the people were all willing to
assist him. So two of the gentlemen went round
with their hats, and collected 30 or 40 dollars,
besides some tea and sugar, which were given me.
They also paid my passage home. We stopped
at Cape Cod on our return, and staid two or three
days where I distributed tracts from house to house.
At that time there was a glorious reformation
here; the Rev. Mr. Lincoln was their minister.
From thence I shipped with Capt. Colman of Cape
Cod, at whose house I had staid while I was there,
and arrived safely at Deacon Spencer's, at Had-
lyme, a parish in East Haddam on Connecticut
river. Deacon Spencer was so kind as to send
me home in his chaise. I arrived at home, and
in September there was a great revival in Litchfield, Conn. I wanted to go there very much, but
was afraid to undertake to ride so far on horseback;

so Dr. Lyman's daughter took her father's chaise, and carried me to Litchfield, to the house of her uncle, the Rev. Daniel Huntington. Here I had a happy time of it; stayed some time, and went and visited the prisoners in the county gaol, and gave them good tracts, and talked to them. One of the prisoners had been sentenced to Newgate. The last of October I returned and spent the winter at home.

CHAPTER XI.

The next March I was looking unto God to direct me what I could do for his glory and the good of my fellow men; and while lying on my bed, all at once the words came very powerfully to my mind, recorded in Isa. lv. 10th, 11th. I took my bible and read the chapter. Soon as I could, I got ready, and went to Connecticut river, on board of a sloop bound to New York. All the money I had in the world was two dollars and twenty three cents. I paid one dollar for my passage, and one dollar for my board, and then had but twenty-three cents when I arrived at New York. I went to Rev. Dr. John B. Romeyn's, and

6*

tendered my services to the Bible Society. The doctor asked me how far I would go. I told him to Philadelphia. So the churches at New York sent seven letters by me; and the day I was going to start, just as I was getting into the stage, my friends handed me twenty dollars to pay my way. I arrived in Philadelphia the 23d of March, and went to see Robert Ralston, Esq., where I dined with the London missionaries bound to India. Mr. Ralston let me have twenty-four bibles and some tracts. I had one hundred tracts of Mr. Malcoo, and four bibles, three testaments, and a number of other good books of a Female Society. I left Philadelphia the afternoon of the 27th of March, in the mail stage, and arrived at New York the next morning. I there received twenty-four bibles and two hundred tracts of the New York Bible Society, then took leave of my friends, and shipped on board the sloop Juliet, Capt. Thomas Fuller, master, and arrived home the 17th day of April. I found my family well. I then went to Boston, and requested the Bible Society to let me have some bibles to distribute. They gave me twenty-four bibles which I brought home on horseback.

The 17th of June, 1811, I went to Farmington, to meet the General Association and ask their advice where I had better go to distribute the books. They all as one said, to the state of Rhode Island.

I then went back to Hartford, and got twenty-four bibles of the Connecticut Bible Society, and now had bibles from four different states but no conveyance, to go with them through the country, and no money to buy a waggon and harness. I kept looking to God for direction, and that he would open a door for me, and blessed be his holy name, I did not look in vain. My worthy brother Normand Smith and Henry Pratt purchased a waggon and harness that cost sixty dollars and told me I might use them six months, and they would trust my master for the pay. I then took my horse with the waggon and bibles I had received in Hartford, and drove home. In a day or two I went to New Haven to the Rev. Mr. Merwin's, and he went with me to the Tract Depository, and they let me have 600 tracts. I got home the 4th of July, and was very much fatigued by reason of the heat. I remained at home till the 24th of July, and then started for the state of Rhode Island with 97 bibles, 3 testaments, and 2000 tracts. I rode to Norwich, and put up with the widow Lathrop—drove the next day to Providence to Rev. Thomas Williams, who lodged with a Mr. Parker, one of the tutors of the college. The next day was the Sabbath; so I went to meeting, and spent the day very agreeably. The next day Mr. Williams went with me to Mr. Walter Paine's, one of the deacons of his church, and also to Governor Jones'. When the Governor had read my letters, he took me by the hand and bid me welcome to their corrupt state. So the Governor gave me several notes to the judges of the courts, and one to Lieut. Gov. Owens, who lived in Gloucester.

I then went to Johnstown factory, owned by Judge Lyman and others, where there were fifty people at work. I supplied them with bibles, and the youth with tracts; and then went to Warwick, where I found five cotton factories. Here I supplied the parents with bibles, and the children with tracts, but found numbers that could not read. I put up at Warwick with Mr. John Allen, and spent the first sabbath in August with him; heard elder Curtis preach, and was pleased with him. In the afternoon Mr. Curtis told the people to meet him and me at the back side of the meeting-house, where I would distribute bibles and tracts. So they came together and I gave books and tracts to them that were needy.

The next day, the 6th of August, I rode to Coventry, and thence to West Greenwich, and put up with Judge Nichols. Here I found the greater part of the people at a funeral. There had been a man and his son drowned the *sabbath day* before, while they were at work taking clams. As the people were returning from the funeral, I stopped under a tree, and got out a number of tracts, and gave one to each as they came along by. The next day, August 7th, I rode to East Greenwich; on my way called on Judge Johnson, who treatea me very kindly, and got up his horse, and rode to East Greenwich with me. I put up there with Mr. Richard Madison; visited elder Manchester, who waited on me the next day, and went with me from house to house to see who, might be in want of bibles. I gave notice to those that were needy to meet me at the Court House, at 4 o'clock, P. M. They came together, and I told them how the Lord had sent them those bibles by the instrumentality of the Bible Societies.

The next day I rode to Wickford, a seaport town; put up with Judge Tillinghast, and went round from house to house with Elder Thurber. I supplied six families that we found destitute of the Bible. On Monday, August 13th, I shipped on board a packet for Newport, and was put across the water 15 miles, to Newport, at free cost, by the judge and Mr. Garner, cashier of the bank at Wickford. All this time as I had been riding through the state I was an utter stranger, but God was pleased to make me many friends. At Newport I took leave of the captain of the packet and his men, who treated me more like godly men than like sailors, and rode to a Mr. Garner's, out of town. I put up with him until the next day; visited the Rev. Mr. Tenney, then at Newport,

and the Rev. Dr. Patton, who treated me so ten-
derly that I melted down like a child that had been
lost and had found his father. O what a glorious
meeting I had with him. Now I could speak
freely with my own dear brethren, for before I had
been with six different kinds of Baptists.

I spent the day with Mr. Tenney and Dr. Pat-
ten consulting where it was best for me to
go next. They had received two hundred bibles
from Boston for that place, and so they thought it
best that I should go to Warren, north of Newport,
and south of Providence.

I had a bad river to cross, and arrived at Warren, just at night. I put up with Elder Baker, a
Baptist, who told me he did not wish me to leave
any of my bibles at that place. He was opposed
to doing anything that should help me, or the
poor of the town. I asked him if there were not
some poor people there. He said he did not know
of any. I told him our Lord had said, " Ye have
the poor always with you, but *me* ye have not always." I next rode to Bristol, called on the Rev.
Mr. White, and stayed with him two days and
two nights. Visited the poor and supplied the
needy with bibles. Mr. White has had to fight
the bulls of Bashan there for twenty years, and he
has fought like a good soldier of Christ. The 18th
of August I rode to Barrington, put up with a Mr.
Watson, one of the standing order; spent the

sabbath with him, and on Monday, the 20th visited and supplied the needy with bibles. Thence, rode to Providence; thence to Pawtucket; called on Elder Benedict, visited his poor, and supplied them with bibles and tracts, and rode from thence to Capt. Stone's cotton factory, on the Gloucester road, three miles north of Providence. Here I found a number of poor whom I supplied.

I had now but two bibles and a few tracts left. So I rode from Capt. Stone's to a place called Tophet, which was a nickname given to it for its wickedness. Here I distributed some tracts and the two bibles I had left, and as I was now out of books, I set off for home. Came to Plainfield, and put up with Dr. Benedict; and the next day to Norwich, where I put up with Capt. Perkins, Cashier of the bank, and a godly man. The next day I got home, and found all my family well.

CHAPTER XII.

I now looked to God for direction what to do, and where to go next, that I might get more bibles; and his holy majesty soon directed, and I went to New York the first of October, 1811—visited my friends there and told them of my success. Dr. Romeyn gave me a line to the Bible Society for sixty bibles for the poor of Rhode Island. At the same time I had some presents from my friends. I put up my bibles, and sailed for home, and arrived at East Haddam, the 27th day of October. The first of November, I rode to Boston, and gave my friends a statement of my doings the summer past; went to the Bible Society, and they offered me three hundred bibles, but I could not carry them for want of a stouter horse. So I took one hundred bibles, (twenty of

7

them of the larger kind, and fifty testaments— also, two thousand tracts, and some other bound and half bound books, put in my hands by Mr. Walley, for the poor of Rhode Island. Mr. Walley and his lady also advanced me twenty-five dollars to help me to get a stouter horse. From Boston I rode to Providence and stored the books with Gov. Jones until the next spring.

Took my leave of the Governor who seemed to be truly pleased to see me so much engaged in such a good cause—rode for home—and arrived at East Haddam the 14th of November.

The first of April, 1812, I rode to Hartford, and got one hundred bibles and some testaments, and some other books of Messrs. Hudson and Goodwin; came home and set off again for Rhode Island. Rode to Norwich and put up at the Pilgrim's house, that is to say, at the man of God's, Capt. Hezekiah Perkins.

April 21, drove to Westerly, and put up with Mr. Thomas Perry, cashier of the Washington Bank. The next day I went out and supplied the poor that wanted with bibles.

The next day rode to Judge Hoxey's, at Washington, and supplied them that wanted. Thence, rode to Little Rest, put up with James Helm, Esq., and the next day visited the poor, and went to the Jail to see the prisoners, and gave them some bibles and tracts.

The next day rode to Wickford, put up with Mr. John Tenent, supplied the poor with bibles and tracts. Thence rode to Warwick, where elder Curtis was the preacher, a man of liberal education, and one who took great pains to find out those who were in want of bibles. In that part of the town there were three cotton factories. We gave notice that Bibles and tracts would be distributed at the meeting house on the Lord's day. So I put the books and tracts into my waggon, and after the meeting I was ready to distribute them to the poor. We had a roll of the names of those who were to have them, and so I distributed thirty one bibles and three hundred tracts. It was a pleasant time to see some poor colored people rejoicing and praising God that he had put it into the hearts of some of his dear children to send them the Bible. I felt very happy in my mind, and thought I was well rewarded for all my trouble. It almost overcame me to see some whose souls, I had great reason to believe, had been purchased by the blood of the glorious Son of God, with their eyes all in a flood of tears, looking up to heaven for me and praying that God would reward me for my labor of love to them and their children.

That evening I went to a conference meeting, with elder Curtis, where deacon Shaws, of his church exhorted the people to make a good use

the bibles which I had given them. "For my own
part," said he, "if I had not a bible, I should not
dare to take one, the charge that brother Burke
has given is so solemn. It would be better, my
friends that we had been born blind than to have
the bible put into our hands and not to make a
good use of it."

The next day, April 27th, as all the bibles and
testaments which I had brought with me were
gone, I went to Providence to get those which I
had brought from Boston, and left with Governor
Jones the fall before.

It was a training day ; the Foot and the Light
Horse were parading in the street, and the drums
beating, and the colors flying, so that I could
hardly keep my horse still. Governor Jones went
with me to his store, and helped me to load the
books. They were in a pine box, and in canvass
bales but we put them into my travelling trunk,
which was large enough to hold three hundred
bibles. I gave the Governor many thanks for his
brotherly love to me, and for his kindness to the
poor of the state, and then rode to Johnstown, put
up with Mr. Manton, and supplied those that
wanted, with bibles and tracts.

April 28. I rode to Judge Lyman's Factory and
distributed ten bibles, 18 testaments, and a number of tracts to the workmen. Went home with
the judge, and the next day rode to Gloucester,

twenty-two miles from Providence; put up with Lieut. Gov. Owens, who gave me all the assistance that he could. Here I visited the schools, and gave the children Emerson's catechism, and supplied the parents with bibles and testaments.

The next day, April 30, rode to Smithfield Factory, and put up with Capt. John Slater. I had to ride thirteen miles through the woods, and had a good deal of trouble to find the way. I found four or five hundred people at work in Capt. Slater's factory. I distributed twenty-one bibles, four testaments, and a number of tracts among his people, and the next day, May 1, rode to Bartlett's factory, where I distributed five bibles and four testaments, and rode from thence to Pawtucket. Here I put up with Mr. Walker, and stayed with him from Friday till the next Monday. Elder Benedict went round from house to house with me, and we found there were twenty-nine who needed bibles or testaments. So we carried the books to the meeting house, Sabbath afternoon, and distributed them to those who needed. I also gave a number of Doddridge's four sermons on the education of children, to the parents.

Monday, May 5. I rode to Boston; put up with Rev. Joshua Huntington, reported my doings to the Bible Society, and also made a statement concerning the situation of the churches and people in Rhode Island. I visited Gov. Phillips and

7*

his son-in law, Mr. Walley; received some bibles
and testaments, and then rode to Coventry in the
western part of Rhode Island. I arrived there
on Saturday night, and put up with Mr. Love.
The next morning, some of his neighbors who
knew I had bibles and testaments to distribute,
came in, and I supplied them that needed; and
conversed with them about the one thing needful.
Mr. Love asked me to pray with them, and so I
did, and gave them some tracts called the "Swear-
er's Prayer."

I then went to meeting in Sterling, Conn., and
the next day set out for home by way of New
London. There I had a good visit with General
Huntington, and thence I came to East Haddam,
and found my family well.

CHAPTER XIII.

Continues the distribution of bibles and tracts. Third visit to Rhode Island. Determines to visit the destitute parts of New York and Pennsylvania. Providentially provided with money for the journey. Goes to Greenbush and visits the soldiers in the barracks. Goes to Albany and Saratoga. Sets out for the Susquehanna river.

I kept on in this business through that summer. Received a load of bibles and tracts at Hartford, which I distributed in Connecticut and some parts of Massachusetts. Returned home in September, and the first of October went to New York and got a quantity of bibles and other good books. At this time, one of the elders of Dr. Romeyn's church put into my hands one hundred and thirty of Stoddard's Guide to Christ that I might give them to the youth.

I sailed for home with a blessed cargo of books, arrived safely, and I hope praised God for my success in so good a cause. I then set off again for Rhode Island, and travelled through the state as usual, and kept exhorting those that were able to form a Bible Society. I found Gov. Jones would do all he could to forward such an undertaking, and requested him to lay it before the Assembly. He did so, and told them how much pains his poor friend Burke had taken to bring them bibles from the other states without fee or reward. I used to tell them that I would keep on till they should form a Bible Society of their own. They did this soon after, and I then turned my attention to the wilderness of New York state, and Pennsylvania.

I had been for five summers in Rhode Island, and through Connecticut in the spring and fall.

So in the spring of 1818, I went to Hartford, and requested to have two hundred bibles to carry to the destitute parts of New York. So the Young Men's Bible Society let me have the number, besides which the Rev. Abel Flint gave me a great number of pamphlets. I then came home, and went to Boston, where I got as many more. I then returned home and prepared to set out on my long journey. The Rev. Dr. Lyman came to see me before I started, and he, knowing I was poor, asked me how much money I had; I told him fifty cents. He asked me if it would not be presumption for me to venture out with so small a sum. I told him *the Lord would provide.* So I set off on the first day of June, 1816, and rode to Hartford, where one lady handed me seven dollars, and several other of my friends gave me more or less. So when I stopped at noon and counted my money, I found I had twenty dollars. *So we see the Lord can provide.*

I went on from Hartford towards Albany, till I came to Greenbush, where I put up with Mr. Cone, from East Haddam, whose dear mother was a member of our church. She was glad to see me with such a number of good books for the poor of that state. Here were six or eight hundred soldiers in the barracks, and I had a friend there, Lieut. Ransom, of Hartford. I asked him to get leave for me from the commanding officer to distribute bibles and tracts, among the soldiers. So the officer gave me leave to come to the barracks, and I gave bibles and tracts to those of the soldiers that wanted. I spent the Sabbath with Mr. Cone, and went to meeting over the river, at Albany. On Monday, I went to see Mr. Boardman, one of the elders of Rev. John Chester's church; stayed with him two nights, then left part of my load, and rode to Saratoga springs, where I found a fine field for the distribution of Bibles and tracts. I then returned to Albany, and the Rev. Mr. Chester put sixty bibles and several other good books into my waggon. The dear brethren at Albany treated me very kindly. I now left them, and set off for the Susquehanna river, one hundred miles by the way of New Durham. I called on the Rev. S. Williston, at New Durham, who was rejoiced to see me with such a stout horse and good new waggon, and a great strong trunk that would hold four hundred bibles, and more than six thousand tracts and pamphlets, which I carried in a large canvass bag. It rejoiced his holy soul to see it, and I stayed with him over the sabbath. He also put some volumes of sermons into my hands. From thence I went on till I came to Wattle's Ferry, on the Susquehanna river. The bridge was so rotten that it was unsafe to cross upon it; so Col. Johnson very kindly took his horse, and rode six miles with me as a pilot, to cross the Unadilla bridge, and to introduce me to the Rev. Mr. Chapin and children. Here I was at home with this man of God and his dear wife and children. So after I had rested, we took two large saddle bags, filled them with bibles and tracts, and set off on horseback, on a mission through the wilderness on the road to Bath. We found good custom for our bibles and tracts. We were gone one night, which we spent at Oxford. We put up with the Rev. Mr. Thorp, one of the standing order, whose wife and two daughters were excellent singers. He sent for some of the young ladies of the place who were singers, and we had a very pleasant meeting. The next day we set out for home by another route, where we found many who were needy, and who were highly pleased with the Bibles and tracts which we

gave them. We arrived at Mr. Chapin's before
night, and the next day I parted with him. It
gave me a heavy heart to take leave of so good a
man. Now I was once more in the wilderness, but
I trust God was there, and that he was my pilot.
I kept on through the country, till I came to the
township of Windsor. Here I found a man by
the name of Harpford, who had been twenty-two
years a professor in the college of New York.
He was European born, and was now eighty-five
years old, and a very godly man. I put up with
him one night; his wife was dead, and one of his
daughters kept house for him. He gave me all
the advice that he could about my route, and when
I got ready to start he went to his desk, and handed me eight silver dollars, with his blessing. He
also charged me to call on his son's wife, five
miles on the road. I then went forward, calling
at every log-house I came to, to see who was in
want of bibles and tracts. When I came to Mr.
Harpford's son's house he was gone, but his wife
was at home, and when I found her, *I found a
good woman.* So she called a boy to cut some
grass for my horse, and I stayed to dinner. Two
poor women came there, and she requested me to
give each of them a bible which I did. She told
me she came from Sharon, in Conn., and when I
showed her my credentials signed by Governors
Phillips, Jones, and Cotton Smith, she told me

she knew Gov. Smith, of Sharon, Conn., and when I left her she gave me five dollars.

I now went on towards the centre of the township, which was twenty miles square, and put up near the meeting house, with David Hotchkiss, Esq., a man of seventy-eight, formerly from Connecticut.

The appearance was that I should want more bibles here than I had. Their minister gave notice that there was an agent from the Bible Society, with bibles for the poor, and the people flocked together from all parts of the town. One woman came twenty miles, and I gave her a bible with pleasure. Two sisters also came five miles over a large mountain that stood on the east or opposite side of the Susquehanna river; at the river they could not get across, till they found an old canoe which they paddled over themselves. This was of a Thursday, and a very rainy day, and when these two sisters told me of their journey over the mountains and across the river, my heart leaped for joy to think that I could give each of them a bible and some tracts. In this place I distributed nearly a hundred bibles and testaments, and two or three hundred tracts. I stayed here three days and a half, and when I was to go away, my friends told me I must have a pilot, or I could not find the way. There was no road nor path but by trees marked, and there was a great mountain to cross four miles in width. So my dear brother Hotchkiss took his horse and rode before me through the woods, and if my horse had not been very stout, I would never have got over the mountain.

When we got as far as we talked of before we set out, I told the squire I was afraid I should get lost; so the good man kept on with me till we came to a settlement where he was acquainted. There we called on Capt. Hawley, a brother who treated me well; and after dinner, my dear brother Hotchkiss wished me success, and took his leave to return home. He also gave me two dollars to help me along. He was a good friend to the Bible cause.

8

CHAPTER XIV.

Goes to Silver Lake. Difficulties and perils in his journey. Crosses the Susquehanna at Keeler's ferry and comes to Wilkesbarre ; thence to Philadelphia. Applies to Mr. Girard in behalf of some ladies at Wilkesbarre. Returns through New Jersey. Visits Dr. Boudinott. Laid up at Princeton with a swelling. Visits Rockaway. Sudden death of Elder Crane.

Here was another good field to distribute bibles. The next day I set off for Silver Lake, in the north eastern part of Pennsylvania. At the village of Montrose I found a Mr. Foster, from Long Island, who was a good brother. I got to his house on Friday, and stayed with him and his partner over night. His partner was from Connecticut. They were merchants in the village. They wanted me to send them a young man that was a preacher, as they had no preacher in the place. Throughout this journey, as it was a very wet summer, I found the roads in this part of the country very bad and miry. Some of the ground was clay, and the road would be like mortar. I suffered great hardships, and my horse also; for as the crops had all been cut off the summer before, I could get neither hay nor oats.

I left Mr. Foster and my friends, and set off for the village of Tunkhannock, which lay on the road to Keeler's Ferry, on the Susquehanna river. This was on the 22d of July. Here it was that I dreaded the route, as there had been several robberies committed there, and not a house to be seen for a great many miles. I tried to get a pilot, but could not; so I looked up to God that he would be pleased to guide me in the right way. I rode through the woods and swamps, which wearied me and my horse very much, as neither of us could get any thing to eat. So I stopped a few minutes to let my horse rest. It was so warm, and I was so faint for want of food, that I was obliged to sit in the waggon, although I would sooner have carried the horse and waggon myself if I had strength. I now drove on slowly, till I came to a very great slough, which was like a bed of mortar. It would have been very hard for a fresh horse to get through it.

I kneeled down by the side of the waggon and prayed to God to strengthen me in body and soul. I pleaded the promises with tears in my eyes, and when I got through I can safely say that if I had eaten the best dinner in the world, I should not

have felt stronger. I stood up a few seconds astonished at my strength, and then took the reins
in my hand, and the horse went directly through
the slough with as much ease it seemed as if the
waggon had been empty. When I got across I
looked up to God, and gave thanks. I now got
into the waggon, and drove a few miles, when I
saw the Susquehanna river. I soon after saw
the village of Tunkhannock, where I had a line
to the widow McCurdy, a pious lady, rich in faith,
and rich as to property. I went to her house and
gave her the line from one of her Christian friends.
She received me very kindly, and wished me to
put out my horse, and remain with her; and as it
was about four o'clock in the afternoon, I did so,
and found every thing plenty and good. After tea
I showed her my travelling letters, to let her know
that I was not an imposter. She read them with
pleasure, and bid me welcome to her house. Soon
we began to look around for those that were in
need of bibles; the next day supplied them that
wanted, and in the afternoon bade the good woman farewell, and rode to Keeler's Ferry, twenty
miles. I had to cross the Tunkhannock Narrows,
where the ends of three mountains all come to
the river. They looked like the clouds, and were
right up and down over the river. When I got to
the top of one of them and looked down, it put me
in mind of Capt. Riley's description of the place
*8

where the Arabs met the Jews, where one must lie down and let the other step over him, or else turn off over the precipice. The river seemed to be as much as fifty or sixty rods from where the waggon was; the road was cut through the rocks, and was not more than seven or eight feet across; and if any other waggon had met me we could not have passed by each other possibly. But God was pleased so to order it that I met none till I had crossed all the three mountains. When I had got across them, I hope I was thankful. I then rode on to Keeler's Ferry, and he put me across the river for nothing. He was very glad to see me with such a cargo. I supplied his family with tracts. I then went for Kingston, where the Indians killed so many of the New England people during the revolutionary war. Here I found a Mr. Harding, from Colchester, in Conn., and put up with him, and stayed two days. My horse was very poor, but here was plenty of forage, and he soon recruited. I supplied the poor with bibles and tracts, and went for deacon Hoyt's, a brother of the Rev. Mr. Hoyt, now a missionary to the Cherokee Indians.

I arrived at the deacon's about sunset, and was kindly received by him and his family. The news soon went to Wilkesbarre, where his brother then preached, but he was gone at that time to Harrisburgh, to get contributions to bear his expenses to Brainard. I supplied those that wanted bibles.

Here I found a Mr. Buckingham, a merchant in Kingston, who took great pains to assist me. The Lord reward him for it. He had my horse shod at his own expense, and made me some presents besides. The deacon and he were very anxious to have me stay, and go to Wilkesbarre, and spend the sabbath, and attend meeting with Rev. Mr. Hoyt's people. So on Saturday night Mr. Hoyt's daughter came to her uncles, the deacon, and I got up my horse, and went across to Wilkesbarre, and spent the sabbath with the church and people there. I carried my own bible and psalm book with me during all my travels. I found that there was a mixed multitude of people at Wilkesbarre, of Dutch, Yankees, and Buckskins, and a great deal to do. So on Monday I went from one part of the settlement to another, and supplied them that wanted, with bibles, testaments and tracts. Here I found two young men who had escaped from Bonaparte's army, in France, and I gave each of them a French bible, as I had some French bibles with me. They were very steady young men, and had a good character among the people. I visited all the gaols I came across in my travels, and conversed with the prisoners about the one thing needful. The gaolor in this place asked me to come and attend meeting with the

prisoners. So I told him I would come the next
day in the afternoon, at 6 o'clock. So when I
came he took the prisoners out into the yard,
under a large apple tree. They were ten in number, four of whom were criminals, one for coun-
terfeiting on the bank of the United States—the
other three for robbery. These four were loaded
with chains. It made me feel very tender to see
them. The inhabitants flocked in, but the gaolor
would not let them come very near. So I went
to prayer with them, and then read the 23d chapter of Luke, and made some remarks on the 40th,
41st, and 42d verses. I talked very plain to them
for I had been to see them twice before. Three
of them were to have their trial the next Monday ;
six of them were brothers, who had been in state
prison six months for robbery, and werenow going
to be tried for the second offence of the same kind.
I exhorted them to repent, and told them Christ
was as willing to forgive them as he was the thief
on the cross. The man that had counterfeited
was deeply affected and told me he would gladly
see me again if he could. I then took my leave
of them, and the gaolor, and as this was Saturday, the next Monday I set off for Philadelphia. I
went by the way of the Green mountain ; the distance was one hundred and thirty miles, and forty
miles of it was as lonely a road as I ever travelled ;
thirty miles of it was a log turnpike ; this lay be-

tween Wilkesbarre and the Green mountain; so
that when I heard a cow-bell, or the barking of a
dog, I would rejoice in hopes to see some human
being. So in the afternoon I came to two or three
log houses, where I called to see if they wanted
bibles. I found they did, and so I supplied them,
and also gave them tracts. Just before sunset I
came to the Green mountain, where I put up with
a Dutchman for whom I had a letter from Mr.
Buckingham, to have him keep me at free cost,
and he would pay him the next time he came that
way. So the good old Dutchman kept me, and
the next morning I set off for Germantown, on
the way to Philadelphia. I was now out of books.
I arrived at Philadelphia the 22d day of August.
I had a letter from the Female Society at Wilkesbarre, to Mr. Stephen Girard, the rich Frenchman,
to send them some money to help them to hire a
preacher, as Mr. Hoyt was going to leave them to
be a missionary among the Indians. This Mr.
Girard kept a bank of his own, with a capital of
seven millions of dollars. So I put my horse to
stable, and put up myself with my good sister
Catharine Hall, where I put up when I went to
Philadelphia after bibles, seven years before. The
next day I visited Robert Ralston, Esq., who was
glad to see me, and hear me tell of my journey.
I asked him for some bibles to carry to Rockaway,
in the state of New Jersey. So he gave me an

order for twenty-five bibles, and twenty-five testaments.

I then went to see Mr. Girard, at his house, but
he was at his bank; so I went there and gave
him the letter. When he had seen the ladies'
names he told me he did not know them, and
that he had not time just then to read the letter,
but I might call on him at twelve o'clock, in Water street, and he would then give me an answer.
So I called on him at the time, and his answer
was, " *I can't do any thing about this business.*"

I visited Mr. Malkoo, who had put a number of
tracts into my hands when I was at Philadelphia
the first time. He gave me two guineas. There
was a great revival in the church to which he belonged. I spent the sabbath with him, and on the
sabbath noon he and myself went three miles
into the country, to visit a sabbath school, and
then returned to the meeting. After tea a young
clergyman came to his house, who was going to
preach that evening in the Female Academy. So
he and the young minister, when they had seen
my letters, thought it would be best for me to tell
my experience, as there would be a great many
young people at the meeting, and he would inform
them that he wished me to tell it rather than to
preach himself.

So I gave him my letters and we went. The
academy had two rooms, and a swinging partition.

I should judge there were three or four hundred people present that night. So the young minister told them he had some letters in his hands, and an account of a man's conversion such as he never heard of, except some accounts in the bible. The man who owns these letters is a Mr. Burke, who sits here by me, and if it be your mind that he should tell his experience instead of my preaching, I shall take your silence for consent. He then read a psalm, which was sung; then he prayed, and then he read the letters, which opened a door for me to begin. So I gave a full statement of all that took place concerning me, and of the great change that I experienced. There were very few present, young or old, who were not in tears. After this they sung again, and the young minister asked me to make the concluding prayer.

The next morning, Monday, August 27th, I set out for Burlington, in New Jersey. Called on Dr. Boudinott, to know where I might find a book called the "Star in the West," written by him some time ago to show that the Indians on this continent were a part of the ten tribes of Israel. Dr. Boudinott was confined to his room with the gout, but he sent for me to walk up stairs. I told him who I was, and showed him my letters. He said he should be very happy to have me stay and spend the night with him, which I did. I found him to be a pious, humble Christian. Before I left him he gave me a check on the Bank for ten dollars, and also the " Star in the West," and another book called the "Anti-Christian Confederacy."

I then rode to Princeton, and stopped at the public house kept by Mr. Hamilton. I had a swelling on my limb, and did not feel able to go any farther till it should be removed. So when the Rev. Mr. Schenck heard of me, he sent and had me carried to his house, and took the best care of me and my horse. He sent for his family physician, who visited me at free cost; he was one of the elders of the church. A number of the pious students also came to see me, and gave me some money. Here I could see how God will order all things in mercy, to them that put their trust in him.

When I got able to walk I went to see Dr. Miller, and Dr. Alexander, to request them to send a candidate to Montrose, and another to Wilkesbarre, which they promised to do. I was in Princeton two weeks. I then rode for Newark, where I put up with Dr. Griffin, who gave me a line to the Rev. Mr. King, of Rockaway, where there was then a great revival. I then went to Rockaway, and when Mr. King found out who I was, and what I was doing, he was very glad to see me. The next day he sent a young man to pilot me through the woods to a furnace, and gave me a letter to the foreman. So after dinner I went to the furnace, and gave the workmen some bibles and testaments, and then returned to Mr. King's that night, and attended a conference in the evening.

I stayed there two nights, and then rode to Caldwell, where a Mr. Grosvenor preached, who came from Windham, Conn. I had a letter for Mr. Bates, brother in law of Mr. King. So I went there, and the next day, being the Sabbath, I went to meeting, and Mr. Bates introduced me to Mr. Grosvenor. He asked us over to his house, and as we were sitting there, in the piazza, Mr. Bates and one of the elders of the church were saying something about the uncertainty of our lives, and asked me what I thought of it. I told them there were six of us on that seat then; that we had all seen the sun rise that morning, but it was uncertain whether we six should all live to see the sun set that night. So the subject passed off; the bell rang for afternoon meeting; Mr. Grosvenor came out to go, and we six walked along after him. Just as we got to the end of the meeting-house, there was a willow tree, and a number of horses tied under it. Elder Crane, one of the six that had been speaking of the uncertainty of life just before, left us and walked up to one of the horses for something, and the horse kicked up with

9

both his hind feet, and struck elder Crane in the pit of the stomach so violently that he died in three quarters of an hour. It was a solemn time that afternoon with us all.

CHAPTER XV.

The next day I rode to New York, where I stayed three days; got some bibles and tracts, and then went to Long Island, where I spent about two weeks and found many excellent people. The first night I put up with James Weeks, Esq., of Jamaica, a member of Congress. The next day I visited Mr. Weed, the minister, and went from house to house, to give bibles and tracts to those that wanted.

The next place I visited was Hempstead, where they come from the South to run horses. Here was an Episcopal clergyman, the Rev. Mr. Lyman, and a Presbyterian, the Rev. Mr. Webster. I distributed ten or twelve bibles, and a number of tracts. This was a dark spot in respect to Christian knowledge. From Hempstead I went to

the north side of the Island and visited the Rev.
David Bogert, a real gentleman and Christian.
I spent some time there visiting among his people, and then returned to Jamaica. There I received a letter from my daughter, with the intelligence that her mother was not likely to live. I
hastened to New York, and from thence set off,
and came directly home to East Haddam. When
I arrived the neighbors were all coming in to see
her, and it was thought she was then dying. But
she revived again. As soon as I came in she
knew me, and said she was going to leave me.
I then kneeled down by the bed-side, and went to
prayer with her. I arrived at home the second
day of October, 1818, and she continued till the
10th day, at 12 o'clock, A. M., when she died.
The day before she died, she asked me to call the
family together, into the room where she was,
and read the 14th of St. John's gospel. It was a
great comfort to me and my children. She was
very happy in her mind during the whole of her
sickness, and in death she breathed out her soul
as if she had been going to sleep.

Here I was left a mourner with eleven children,
with but very little of this world for our support.
But the Lord has wonderfully provided for them
and me, and blessed be his holy name for it.

The Rev. Dr. Lyman preached the funeral sermon at the burial of my wife, from the sixth verse of Jude. He preached from the same text the first time my wife and I ever heard him preach, which was thirty-two years before.

9*

CHAPTER XVI..

Second marriage. Visit to Boston and Rhode Island and goes to the Blackstone factory, in Massachusetts. Returns home. Next spring goes into Massachusetts and the State of New York. Second visit to Long Island. Goes among the Indians at the east end of the Island. Visits Boston again. Account of a revival in Millington, the place of his residence. Reflections.

I now remained a widower two years, seven months, and seventeen days. I found myself very lonely, and was then married again to Miss Olive Arnold, a sister in the church to which I belonged. She and my first wife had been great friends, and she had been with my wife much in her sickness. I was married the second time May 27th, 1821.

So, having obtained help of God, we continue to this day. Soon after my second marriage, I went to Hartford, and got a supply of bibles and testaments, which I distributed in Connecticut, Massachusetts, and Rhode Island. The first of November, the same year, I went to Boston, visted my friends, and got a supply of bibles; then home, and to New York, where I took in some bibles and tracts. Then came home, and lay by till the next spring. I then went to Rhode Island, and found the Bible Society could not supply all that needed. So I supplied those that wanted. I then visited the Blackstone factory, in Massachusetts, where there were twelve hundred people at work. I went to the house of Col. Eddy, the agent for the factory, and distributed fifty bibles and fifty testaments to the workmen and also a number of the Boston Panoplist, and tracts. The next day, as I was going to start for Boston, Col. Eddy told me that the young people wished me to attend a conference meeting with them that evening. So my horse was turned out, and I went to the throne of grace for direction how to carry on the meeting. I then took my bible and picked out a suitable chapter, to read and to remark upon, and so at night after singing and prayer, I read a chapter, and made some remarks. I farther told the people that they would have to give account unto God, who had been pleased to send them the bibles which they had just received. The young people were very tender. As soon as the concluding prayer was made, I saw some young men going round with their hats for contribution money; this was very unexpected to me, and when Col. Eddy brought me their mite, I was unwilling to take it, for I supposed they were not well able to give. But he said they wished to do something to show their regard for me, and I must take it. So I took the money, four dollars and seventy-five cents, and the next day set off for Boston.

A part of my route lay through a great body of woods. Here I was led to look back upon my mispent life in youth, and renewedly to implore the divine forgiveness. I was on a lonely road, but was very happy in my mind. When I got to the half-way house between Providence and Boston, I put up with Mr. Fuller, an old friend of mine, not professedly a Christian, but very kind to me, and favorable in his charges. The next day I rode to Boston, and put up with Mr. Edward Phillips. He had lately lost his wife, and as he had but little company, he wished me to come and stay with him. It was now seven years since he had often entertained me when I was in Boston. May the Lord reward him for his kindness to a poor brother. I went to the Bible society, and received sixty bibles and some testaments, besides several numbers of the Panoplist, and some books of Mr. Walley, and then came home to East Haddam. I next went to New York, and got sixty bibles and other good books. Came home, spent the winter at home, and the next June went into several parts of Massachusetts, and New York. In Claverock, (N. Y.) the people were mostly Dutch, but they and their children could generally speak and read English. There, and also on what was called Livingston's Manor, I supplied the poor with bibles and tracts. I then kept down on the east side of the North river, and visited all the ministers that came in my way, from Hudson to New York.

I then took what books I had left, and fifty bibles that the good Dr. James Milnor, of the Episcopal church put into my hands, and a quantity of tracts which the Female Tract Society put into my care for distribution, and set off for the east part of Long Island. I went first to Jamaica, and called on James Weeks, Esq. Thence to Hempstead; thence to Quakertown; and from thence to the Rev. Mr. Seabury's, formerly of New London. He treated me like a brother, and gave me directions on the road to Southampton. The road was very difficult to find by reason of the numerous cross roads and paths made by those who transported wood to New York.

At South Hampton, old society, I called on Mr. Babbit, the minister, showed him some letters I had brought from New York, put up with him, and the next day went with him to find who among his people wanted bibles. I stayed there a week, and attended several meetings with Mr. Babbit and his people.

I then rode to Dr. Woolworth's, in the eastern part of the town, who treated me like a good man as he was. Here I found straw and provender for my horse, and good accommodations for myself. I stayed here a while, and made head quarters at the doctor's. He married a daughter of the Rev. Dr. Buell, former minister of East Hampton.

I went from here to Sag Harbour, six miles, in company with Dr. Woolworth, and called on the Rev. Mr. Gardiner, who proved to be a very kind man. He was acquainted all over the Island, and was so good as to give me a list of the names of his and my friends which was of great use to me, as I was an utter stranger in that part of the Island. So the next day I rode to East Hampton, called on the Rev. Mr. Phillips, but he was very busy in harvesting; so he did me neither good nor hurt.

Dr. Woolworth, and I then went to the house of the Widow Gardiner, the widow of Lord Gardiner, Esq., of Gardiner's island. She was an excellent woman, and treated both of us very well. Here Dr. Woolworth left me and returned. So the next day I went as far as I could find inhabitants, on the east end of the Island, and then turned to the south side of the Island, and came to a tribe of Christian Indians. I showed them a letter from the Rev. Mr. Gardiner, as they had a great regard for him. I distributed some bibles and testaments among them and formed some acquaintances. They requested me to stay and attend a meeting with them. So I stayed, and met with them two days in succession, at five o'clock, in the afternoon. We met in their own meeting house, where Paul Cuffee used to preach to them. He was now dead. I went to their burial ground, and saw there a marble monument at the head of his grave, placed there by the Missionary Society of New York. These Indians were generally very fine singers. There was but one white family among them, a Capt. Conklin, who kept a public house, and who treated me very kindly.

I then rode on to the westward, and was most of the time in sight of the ocean. The next place of any note which I came to was ———. Here there was a good house for public worship. I arrived here on Saturday night, and put up with the Widow Foster, one of Mr. Gardiner's friends. One of her son's lived with her in the same house. The whole family were hopefully pious. So the Lord in mercy sent me where I was kindly entertained, and found godly people; and such were very scarce in these parts. The next morning, the Sabbath, I asked young Mr. Foster what they did for a preacher. He said they had no settled minister, but that sometimes Mr. Gardiner, and sometimes Dr. Woolworth came and preached to them. He said they should perhaps have a Methodist preacher that day, but if they did not, they would be glad to have me attend and carry on their meeting. But the Methodist preacher came. I attended his meeting, and he asked me to attend and take the lead in a third meeting, at five o'clock, P. M. So I did, and made some remarks on several portions of scripture. He thanked me for my assistence, and I spent the night very agreeably with him at the Widow Foster's.

The next day I rode to Babylon, on the south side of the island, where I put up with an aged, pious deacon of the Presbyterian church. The next morning, I supplied such as were in want with bibles and tracts. Then proceeeed on till I came again to Hempstead, where I put up with the Rev. Mr. Webster. I stayed with him two or three days, and attended some conference meetings—then rode to Jamaica, where there was now a great awakening. Here I put up with deacon Skidmore; attended conference meetings, and distributed some bibles and tracts.

I then returned to New York, where I stayed a week, and took much satisfaction, going every evening with my friends to some religious meeting. O, 'tis a blessing to be in a part of the world where we can hear the sound of the glorious gos-

10

pel of Jesus Christ, and it is a still greater blessing to have a relish for it.

From New York I returned in safety to my family, at East Haddam, and in a few days went
again to Rhode Island, with some bibles and
tracts which I had just brought from New York.
Visited several factories and supplied them with
books; then rode to Boston; received several
presents from Gov. Phillips and his children;
received a quantity of bibles and other books, then
came to East Haddam, and spent the following
winter at home.

The next September I went to Boston, where
there had been a great revival, and many added to
the churches of Christ; thirty-nine were propoun-
ded while I was there, at one of their meetings
on the sabbath.   I then received some bibles
from Mr. Edward Tuckerman, and a number of
good books from Mr. Evarts.   The Lord reward
him and all my friends who have helped me in
distributing to the necessities of the poor.   The
Rev. Dr. Lyman was dismissed from his people
at Millington, about this time, and when I went
to Boston I tried to find some candidate to supply
the pulpit.   But just then the Lord sent the Rev.
Mr. ———— among us.   There was soon after a
powerful revival at Millington.   Ffty-three of
those who became hopefully pious united with the
church the last sabbath in November, 1823.

Here I had lived twenty-nine years, hoping and waiting for the salvation of the Lord, and now it came. Blasphemers and drunkards were made to bow to king Jesus. The work seemed to put down all the opposition of the enemy. "The Lord hath done great things for us, whereof we are glad;" and I can truly say, "Bless the Lord, O my soul, and all that is within me bless his holy name. Bless the Lord, O my soul and forget not all his benefits."

I have great reason to praise God for his grace to me in times when I knew him not; and great reason to praise Him for his constant goodness towards me, and especially for his permitting me to live till I could see him appear in his glory, to build up Zion in my own dear parish.

But, O my dear reader, what a glorious sight will it be when the prophecy of Isaiah shall be fulfilled, (chapter 60.) When the Light of the Church shall come, and the glory of the Lord be risen upon all the Gentiles. When the sons also of them that afflicted the Church shall come bending unto her, and all they that despised her, shall bow themselves down to the soles of her feet, and shall call her, "The city of the Lord, the Zion of the Holy One of Israel."

That will be a happy day. I do not expect to see it with my bodily eyes; but I do hope to see it from another and a better world, and O such a hope as this makes me young again.   Were it not for such a hope as this, which through the merit and the mercy of the Lord Jesus Christ, has sustained me these seven and thirty years, I should sink.

And when I now see the wickedness of the children of this world, I should sink if I did not know that God will make the wrath of man to praise him. . The sinner will see the justice of God in his own condemnation, since he refuses the pardon which is offered in the gospel.   And O the depth of the riches of Divine mercy to me, who trampled on the blood of Jesus and took the holy name of God in vain a thousand times. Where has mercy ever been so displayed as in the case of William Burke, once a rebel—a prodigal—a great sinner—and wretched and forlorn, but who now stands, and has stood these many years, a Monument of Sovereign Grace.

At the urgent request of Mr. Burke, I have transcribed the foregoing sheets from a manuscript written by himself. My numerous parochial labors have obliged me to do it in the remnants of time, by little and littte. But as it was the wish of Mr. Burke to show his own simple narrative to his Christian friends, I have been careful to copy him as strictly as possible, not only in sentiment but in phraseology. But very few alterations have been made in any part of the Narrative.

Certified by the clergyman who prepared it.

CHAPTER XVII.

His last sickness and death, from a sermon delivered at his funeral by the Rev. Nathaniel Miner, pastor of the church.

The subject of this memoir, died at Millington, May 24th, 1836, in the eighty-fourth year of his age.

The last three or four weeks of his life were a continued scene of extreme suffering; but through it all he appeared like a Christian indeed.

Mr. Burke was born in the county of Galway, Ireland, A. D. 1752. By the death of both his parents he was left an orphan, when not more than nine or ten years old. He was educated in the Roman Catholic religion; but by the grace of God was brought to see the errors of the Man of Sin, and to embrace the doctrines of the Reformation.

At the age of twenty-three, and during the American Revolution, he came to this country, a volunteer in the British army. But soon becoming dissatisfied with the service, he contrived and effected his escape. In 1780 he was married to

Miss Lettice Maynard. By this woman he had twelve children, all of whom survive him, excepting one—the eldest is upwards of fifty, and the youngest more than thirty. His wife experienced religion in about eight years after their marriage, and died in 1818, in a happy and triumphant manner. He was afterwards married to Miss Olive Arnold, who now survives him, to mourn the loss of a kind and affectionate husband.

Mr. Burke experienced religion at Branford, in this state, nearly fifty years ago. Most of the time since his conversion he has spent in this place, and that he has lived an exemplary Christian life, in piety toward God, and benevolence to all men, all who knew him can bear testimony. In ordinary cases, we choose to say but little of the dead; but when a man of such eminent piety is taken away, we may speak more freely. Though we have not regarded the deceased as a perfect man, yet, I believe I do not exaggerate, when I say all have esteemed him as a man of no ordinary excellence. He has been so esteemed by the worst among us.

Since his conversion he has been a warm-hearted and useful Christian. No sooner did he learn the preciousness of Christ, than he sought to lead others to him. For this purpose he travelled in Rhode Island, Connecticut, Massachusetts, New York and Pennsylvania, distributing bibles and tracts to the destitute. Some of those who received bibles and tracts at his hands we believe, are now in heaven. As his heart was much set on advancing the glory of God in the salvation of sinners, he persevered for several years in this work, through many trials and discouragements.

Mr. Burke was a firm believer in the doctrines of grace; God's amiable sovereignty, his wise disposing and controlling all events, was a theme upon which he often dwelt. No one more firmly believed in man's entire native depravity; in his redemption by the atonement of Christ; in the necessity of his regeneration by special grace; and in the perseverence and salvation of all true believers. That the interests of the church were in the hands of Christ; that he could prosper his cause, amid all the degeneracy, darkness and wickedness of the times, and would ultimately fill the world with his glory, were subjects upon which he often dwelt with rapture.

Though he had a comfortable evidence of his union to Christ, yet no one could have a greater sense of unworthiness and dependence. "No one," he would often say, "can get to heaven, but by the help of the blessed Jesus, and no one can come short whom he designs to save."

When told not long before his death of the dying sayings of some good men, and asked what was his, he said—"Since I knew the Lord Jesus, I have had faith in his atonement, as the only way of salvation; this has ever been my comfort, and the ground of my hope. It support-ed me under the loss of my first wife, through the many trials I have since been called to pass, and it supports me under these afflictions, or I should now sink." In his experience, his religious views and feelings, were uncommonly uniform; and be-cause he was uniform and strict in the perform-ance of Christian duty. When a byestander enquired if his faith held out, he replied, "I have had no ups and downs, but since I found the Lord my confidence has been unwavering; it is so now."

His heart was very much set on the ultimate triumph, and universal spreading of the gospel. For this reason, every periodical and pamph-let that contained intelligence of the success of the word of God in any part of the world he per-used with the highest pleasure. For the same reason, he often read those portions of scripture, which speak of the conversion of all nations to Christ. To hasten that glorious period he took a deep interest in all the benevolent institutions of the age.

Besides the funds he often gathered for these, of his small means he gave liberally every year. Of this privilege he would suffer no one to deny him, and what should I say more to his praise,

than at the advanced age of eighty-four he died a
collector of our Bible Society. Though he believed in enlightened Christian effort, he as firmly believed in our dependence on God. Hence he
began and ended all with prayer; in this duty, it
is believed he abounded above his brethren. In
his closet, and in his family, he was truly a man
of God, and many will not soon forget how much
our circles for prayer were enlivened by his earnest and fervent manner. In this duty he was
much engaged during his last sickness. When
he could gain a little respite from pain, he often
engaged in earnest prayer for his own soul, for
his children, and the church of God.

He often entreated the Lord to make him useful
to the very last. " For forty years, (said he,) I
have made it my prayer that God would enable me
to praise and glorify him with my last breath."
This request was mercifully granted. The very
day on which he died he was enabled to speak of
the goodness of God, and to praise him that his
"soul was founded on the Rock of Ages." Among
other traits of excellence, we must not forget to
mention his patience and Christian fortitude.
Though his sufferings were extreme, and for
many days and nights together he could get no
refreshing sleep, yet he bore all without a murmur.
To a Christian brother he said, "These pains and
this struggling for breath, O, it is severe, but when

we remember how much more we deserve than we suffer, our mouths are shut, we cannot complain." At another time he said, "This is trying and severe, but it is nothing to what my Saviour bore for me."

Thus lived and thus died this eminent servant of Christ. When standing at his bed-side, so ripe did he seem for heaven, so ready to depart, we could but say, "My father, my father, the chariot of Israel, and the horsemen thereof." It seemed as if some blessed messenger stood ready to conduct his spirit to heaven.

For his bereaved widow and children, we feel a deep and tender sympathy; but they may be supported by the assurance that what is their loss is his gain. The church to which he belonged will long remember him. To know their loss, they need but remember his ardent love of the brethren; his warm attachment to our beloved Zion; his unshaken confidence in the Redeemer; his fervent prayers and holy example. But few had a warmer heart, but few loved goodness more, but few have desired more the honor of God and the good of his kingdom. "Though I shall not see," he said, " the universal spread of the gospel while in this world, yet I hope to see it when in a better."

THE END.

CPSIA information can be obtained
at www.ICGtesting.com
Printed in the USA
BVHW040051090121
597378BV00027B/258